Dedicated to Jose B. Cisneros

... a gentle soul killed July 12, 1969, in Viet Nam...
We miss you Joe.

© 2018 Howard Fisher
3rd Edition

Howard Fisher
The Living Ghosts
Del Mar to Vietnam, 50th Anniversary 1968-2018

All rights reserved. No part of this publication may be reproduced, stored in a retrieval system or transmitted in any form or by any means, electronic, mechanical, photocopying, recording or otherwise without the prior permission of the publisher or in accordance with the provisions of the Copyright, Designs and Patents Act 1988 or under the terms of any license permitting limited copying issued by the Copyright Licensing Agency.

THE LIVING GHOSTS

"Where the turf meets the surf... to die for."

Del Mar to Vietnam, 50th Anniversary 1968-2018

Writings collected by Rick Griffith
Edited by Weston Fisher

Contents

June, 1968... There It Is
pg. 1

July, 1968... Two Realities
pg. 3

August, 1968... A Duck in a Dog's Kennel
pg. 5

September, 1968... Broken Hail
pg. 10

October, 1968... Hold Your Breath
pg. 15

November, 1968... Here We Go
pg. 18

December, 1968... No One Believed in War
pg. 22

January, 1969... I Can See It All
pg. 26

February, 1969... They Owned the Night
pg. 50

March, 1969... A Picasso in Progress
pg. 80

April, 1969... That Rotten War
pg. 83

May, 1969... Where I can Be Free
pg. 85

INTRODUCTION

In order to make this book Rick Griffith scoured over eight years of social media posts by Howard Fisher. The posts were made when events relating to Vietnam came to Fisher's memory between 2010-2018, the years he's been actively posting on social media. 2019 was the 50th anniversary of Fisher's departure from Vietnam. These posts describe the time leading up to, during, and after his service.

The posts are in order based on the day of the year they were posted to created a time line from Jun - May, roughly covering his journey from beginning to end as it happened from 1968-1969. The posts are not necessarily in order of their happening, but rather when they came to Fisher's memory throughout each year after 2010.

The frequency and subject of the posts offer a glimpse into the workings of PTSD. You'll see that some months have nearly nothing, while others take up the majority of the book. We felt it was important to show them this way.

The posts were edited and organized by Fisher's son, Weston. Only minor edits were made to typo's as Fisher's early social media mastery was still on a learning curve. We felt better to avoid confusion on the readers behalf and correct only specific typos with Fisher's direction. Aside from that nothing has been changed.

Included is an unpublished preface written by Fisher in 2006 following his published article in Vietnam Magazine detailing his injury sustained at L.Z. Grant (which you can read in the back of the book). We've included it to help you better understand the time and place described in Fisher's posts.

Forward

For My Father
By Weston Fisher

Most everything I know of my dad's time in Vietnam has been through his writings. Putting this book together has been an emotional challenge for me. As Howard's son it is difficult for me to imagine him going through what he did both physically and mentally. I've learned so much in the process and am so grateful to have a man like Howard to call my dad. His sacrifice and continuing love for this country are inspirational and heroic.

I've never been able to see my dad's scars the way I'm sure others do. His face is the only way I've ever known it to be. It's just dad. It wasn't until I was an older child that I even knew that other people saw him differently. I'm just so grateful he got out of Vietnam with his life. Some have scars outside, others inside, and some like my dad carry both.

Reading my dad's entries makes me wonder what other great men died in Vietnam and of all the countless people we'll never know. In correcting certain parts of my dad's posts I found it interesting that the one word he consistently misspelled was "tomorrow". All he wanted was to survive L.Z. Grant. So many others did not get so lucky... Tomorrow is never promised in wartime.

Love you, Pop. I'm glad I get to do this for you.

Right: Howard Fisher at LZ Grant, Vietnam

Forward

Preface

This account of combat actions in Vietnam was written by one of the fine soldiers who served during this war. This is his personal story based on what he recalled and learned from contact with others who were there during this action at LZ Grant. I applaud his dedication to his fellow soldiers and telling their stories is important for all Americans to realize the courage and valor of the Vietnam veterans. All combat elements on LZ Grant performed in an outstanding manner and were recognized with unit awards. Howard Fisher is to be commended for his effort to remember his fellow soldiers.

JAMES W DINGEMAN
Colonel (R) US Army
Honorary Colonel-- 12th Cavalry Regiment

Area of Operations: L.Z. Grant
By Howard Fisher   16 October 2006

In June 2006, Vietnam Magazine printed my story about being wounded at L.Z. Grant. That opened many doors for me, which then called for a road trip. My middle son, Travis, had just graduated from High School here in Julian, California and would start Army boot camp on July 25, so we had some time. I met with fellow veterans of L.Z. Grant, in Oklahoma, and Texas, and called one in Colorado, and another in California. I found that the 37 years after the facts, lends strength, to rumors, and half-truths, and to counter that, we fact checked this article, as much as possible. With these and other men's help, I've written our story to honor us, and all who serve America. L.Z. Grant was arguably among Vietnam 's biggest combat stories of 1969. Listen to George Presson, of Ferndale, California, remembering March 11th 1969, *"All our ammo was gone, the ammo dump was empty. We 'd used all our High Explosive, the Beehives, then the "Co Fram", and the NVA (North Vietnamese Army) were still coming through... The command came over the radio to 'fix bayonets' because it looks like things are going to get worse."*

The 1st Cavalry Division (Air Mobile) was one of the many Units of the United States Army in Vietnam. For soldiers assigned to a "Cav" unit, Pride was the Order of the Day. In January 1969, "The Year of the Monkey," three Cav units, deployed together to the area North, and West, of Saigon, toward Cambodia, included were;

Preface

"Charlie" Battery 1st Battalion 77th Artillery
"Alpha" Battery 1st Battalion 30th Artillery
2/12th Cavalry

With a long and glorious history, the 77th Artillery had opened support for the Cav in Vietnam on 16 Sept. 65. The 30th Artillery also has a storied history and their website, www.hardchargers.com, tells "1969 was our hardest year." The 2/12th time "in country" shows that after soldiering through the Que Son Valley, and serving on the outskirts of the City of Hue, then participating at Khe Sanh, the Army relied on these effective, and dependable Infantrymen.

Using the radio call sign, "Birth Control", C -1-77th Artillery was operating with six 105mm Howitzers, manned by crews of five or six "Cannoneers." The Battery staff was Captain Capshaw, SFC/ Chief of Smoke, Rabb, three men in Fire Direction Center (FDC), two cooks, two guys at ammo, and a medic. A/l/30 Artillery also had six big 155 Howitzers, hydraulic power, with crews of six. They were led by LTC Dwight Wilson Battalion Commander, Captain Larry Faust, lSG Tom Vernor, and Chief of Smoke Nonnan Wilfong, all together there were around 120 "cannon cockers" defending L.Z. Grant.

In January '69, the NVA were building up their forces noticeably near the city of Tay Ninh. The 18th of January, the 2/12th's men got the call for a Combat Assault; orders were to re-occupy an old 25th Infantry position, to be named, "L.Z. Grant". Rumors among the men of the 77th were that they were headed to the dreaded "Ho Bo Woods," their sense of relief was short-lived as the soldiers checked out L.Z. Grant.

The view was of flat land, with a road right down the middle of the Landing Zone (L.Z.). There was a major foot trail passing by, which was an NVA supply route, and a stream near the foundation of what once was a French fort. The South end was designated to be the "chopper pad", the North side was the old foundation, so the 155's took the East side of the road, and the 105's, the West. With 120 approximately in the Artillery ranks, and 100 or so Infantrymen on L.Z. Grant, base defense total was near 220.

Outside the wire, men wearing black pajamas were seen, and they obviously were watching the L.Z., they were soon pursued, and some were captured. The NVA POW's said that L.Z. Grant was to be attacked. The plan was said to be; an attack with 120mm rockets, mortars, recoilless rifles, and a charge by NVA regulars, ground troops who were determined to wipe out all the Americans.

These VC (Vietcong) and NVA soldiers were more tolerant of

Preface

Vietnam's conditions in general, than the Americans; still they suffered none the less. They cooked their own chow (rice), and stuffed the extra in socks, tied together, and hung around their necks to eat later. These Vietnamese would often only have a weapon and a web pack, and would be "traveling light." They were ambushed day and night by the 2/12th's soldiers. After engaging the NVA, the GI's would at times find that the survivors had dropped their gear, and run away. The GI's would collect B-40 rockets, RPG's, AK-47's, AK-50's and at least once, a U.S. 50 Cal machine gun. These men were often simply hurrying after their units, and frequently were carrying rice for other hungry NVA.

To counter the NVA presence, the 2/12th kept one line Company on Base Defense, while three line Companies worked the Area of Operation (A.O.), so for Infantrymen, it was one week in, followed by three weeks out. Echo Platoon's mortar crews stayed on Grant. A minority of Infantrymen preferred the "Boonies" to being stuck on an L.Z., but most "Grunts" preferred the break from "humping the boonies". The range of the 105's was 7 miles, for the 155's, almost 9 miles, so that was the A.O.

In Oct 68, Lt Jeffery Andrews of Denver, Colorado, arrived in Vietnam, trained as a Small Unit Commander. Stationed at Quan Loi, he worked supply for the Artillery for the 77th. One day in January of '69 he was reassigned to the field as a Forward Observer (F.O.) to the 2/12th. He left HQ and the 77 and was reassigned to the 2/12th as needed. He was quickly paired up with another soldier, SGT Larry Hutchins of Tishomingo, Oklahoma; Hutchins had been trained as a wheel mechanic and a recon SGT. These two men served together in A. Company from January to September, when Hutchins derosed (date estimated return overseas).

The 2/12th's Companies A, B, C, D, and E, used the radio call signs, "Ace High," "Bad Bet," "Wild Card," "Stacked Deck," and "Easy Winner". These ranks were filled with some of America's best sons. These soldiers came from America's Cities, Towns, and homes in the country. The men were raised to be sophisticated, and in control of their destiny. The GI's in Vietnam were collectively scared of the unknown. Dangers in this foreign land were everywhere, and as for one's destiny, the weapon in your hands was really all you could control. Soldiers were needed who could discern danger, while surrounded by odd smells, plants, and weather. Infantrymen need those among them who make up the "Point Element," GI's who can lead on trails, and look around every curve, while keeping their eyes on the ground, and all else. Some were City boys, never held a rifle before the Army, and they learned fast, as the OJT lessons were daily and deadly, these men were hunters by nature, and these traits can last a lifetime. Men were needed who could stalk, and track, and react instinctively. The GI's needed fellow soldiers up front who were always listening for danger's sounds. In the Company command group, which always walked at minimum behind the lead platoon, of 20 to 30 men, were the likes of Andrews and Hutchins. Hutchins would have the radio, and he and the Lt. were "joined at the hip" says Andrews. Both were NVA targets, Hutchins with the radio, and Andrews because he was an officer, the NVA always had snipers lurking about.

The GI's were hopeful to get a chance to tell the good folks back home about this strange land called Vietnam. To survive, Andrews and Hutchins would have to be able to move fast, and hold still, at almost the same time. One of their first tests came when ambushed in the middle of a mid-day re-supply. A large force engaged the Company and the re-supply chopper immediately took off, men were hit and some chaos broke out as the entire Company retreated to two B-52 bomb craters. Says Andrews, "The fighter jets got us out of that one by napalming around us." he continues, "The 30th was a hell of an outfit, the 77th was the best."

February

The month of February the 2/12th's Radio Telephone Operators (RTO) would call for medical extraction for soldiers with; malaria, heat stroke, fevers, snakebites (bamboo vipers), accidental discharges, bullets, shrapnel, a man goes berserk, bamboo cuts, booby traps, pungi stakes, and some men would be rotated Stateside.

On L.Z. Grants first day, two GI's were driving to the water point when the jeep crunched the plastic top of a 12" hexagonal land mine, two GI's KIA. The unnerving fact was that the mine had been placed unseen and undetected within the past 24hrs; soldiers began to suspect tunnels were beneath the L.Z.

"Bad Bet," or B Company had one WIA on the 1st day of February, he died at the hospital. On February 5th, A, and B Companies, were engaged in day-long contact. That night B Company's ambush engaged 5 NVA, then 30 more, with one GI KIA. All month long the 2/12th's Companies found gear and rice, lots of 50lbs bags of polished rice in enormous amounts, abandoned by the NVA's soldiers who were wary of contact with the 2/12th's angry GI's. The sixth, B Co. again, 1 KIA, 11 WIA, from an unknown source, minutes later, A Co. had 4 WIA, and as they were medevaced there was another KIA and 3 more WIA's. At this rate February was going to be among the worst of times.

The companies rotation in mid-month brought A Co. to base defense for Grant. At this time Hutchins and Andrews may have met the author as occasionally they would visit the Artillerymen and thank them for their work. On the 21st another rotation brought B Company to Grant in time for a heavy mortar and recoilless rifle attack followed by L.Z. Grant's first ground attack. Official stats are 1 American KIA and 7 WIA for 23 Feb. '69. Killed was CPL Jesse Montez of San Antonio, Texas, he died on his 155mm Howitzer. The author was, included in the 7 WIA. See *'Battle for L.Z. Grant' June 2006 VN Magazine.*

Lt. Andrews and SGT Hutchins went through five commanders in their time with A Company. Three were killed. One had command for less than a week, Feb 27, until March 3, the next only lasted 5 days then was killed by gunship rockets on March 8th, the third was inadvertently hit by cannon fire when the helicopter pilots flew into "friendly fire" on June 19th.

March

The battle of February 23rd was in the darkest phase of the moon, two weeks later the nights were bright with moonlight, and NVA rockets were flying on the night of
March 7th. "You could see these little rockets rising up out of the trees, we immediately asked for permission to fire," says George Presson. The first 120mm rocket slammed into the ground next to Echo's men. The second 120mm hit the 155's, and the third hit the road. The next rocket hit directly on the bunker that was the Tactical Operations
center (TOC), and with a delayed detonation, killed most inside. The "grunt's" Commander, Peter L. Gorvad, from Oakland, California, was dead and the NVA were in position to charge the L.Z., ordered to wipe out everybody there.

Even after the loss of the grunt's Commander, there were excellent leaders still alive. Capt Capshaw of the 77th went from Howitzer to Howitzer giving instructions to the crews. He was 20' from gun #5 when smacked down by shrapnel in the back of his helmet. Knocked on his face, he got up, unhurt, and earned numerous decorations at L.Z. Grant. Capshaw's men were using the MI02 model of the105mm Howitzer. The M102 was 2,000 lbs lighter than a regular 105mm and the tail was a joined tail, rather than split tails, this made the guns turnable by hand, and that fact would make a critical difference in this developing battle.

In the dark of the night, the NVA had prepared for this ground attack. Before the attack, for some nights from inside LZ Grant, GI's used Starlight scopes to spot targets, they could see the NVA working in the jungle, and shot at them .The NVA strung several miles of commo wire,

Preface

and connected a ring of organized positions including some Russian .51 Cal machine guns in the tree line encircling Landing Zone Grant's area. The NVA's anti-aircraft gun was seen operating during the battle, and its shells could be heard hitting the passing fighter jets. A direct hit by a 102 reduced the weapon to its gun sight. First the NVA were to mortar and rocket, and then their ground troops were to fanatically charge to finish the killing. Once ready, with the moon three days past full, out of their tunnels poured these Infantrymen dedicated to the NVA.

    One soldier on L.Z. Grant had been on active duty since I 941, since he was fifteen years old. Thomas A. Vernor, from Gautier, Mississippi, started as a gunner in WWII, on a 3 man Torpedo Bomber. He moved into Underwater Demolition Technician by Okinawa, went to China, the Korean War, and served multiple tours in Vietnam. To turn the tide of this battle, Vernor left his bunker that March night, and he crossed the road, leaving his 155mm Howitzers, to commandeer a 102 and its crew. He told the crew, and a soldier from Echo, to bring the beehive rounds and H.E. (High Explosives), and they rolled the 102 down the road toward the chopper pad. NVA troops there were massing for the fanatical charge, and could be seen setting up mortars and guns, in the open. Vernor directed the firing and the beehive rounds were very effective. The Infantry's D Company added their "hot guns", M-60's and small arms along with Echo's mortars, the NVA hardly had a fighting chance. Some NVA carried flame throwers loaded with napalm, and they died within range of the GI's, their flame throwers unused. The 2/12th's popular young SGT Bobby Sanderson, of Barnwell, South Carolina, was medevaced just before dying. The Infantry men held off on using their claymore mines until the enemy was very close, then BOOM, and the human wave crumbled, NVA soldiers piled up quickly. Vernor and crew were aiming and turning the 102's by hand, "If it hadn't been for the 102's... split tails wouldn't have worked. We turned the guns by hand and we had to be fast", George Presson. Vernor still serves America today; this patriot serves as the National Sergeant at Arms Emeritus from the Military Order of the Purple Heart.

    Soldiers on L.Z. Grant had access to newly developed ammo that proved its worth on the next attack of March 11th. The 102's had "Co Fram" which contained in each shell, 18 Bouncing Betty's designed to spread out and explode 10' off the ground. The special ammo for the 155's was called "Firecrackers," or Improved Conventional Munitions (ICM's). At the height of the battle, A-1-30's commander, Capt Larry Faust, and his excellent staff, asked for and received permission to use this ammo, permission was granted from Command by Phil Speairs Battalion's S-3 for 1/30 Arty. Faust and Wilfong signaled the crews to use the ICM's. The first two ICM's completely halted an NVA unit as the shells exploded and sent 38 bomblets out to bounce off the ground and explode at waist height. A cheer began with the 155's soldiers, and was picked up by the 77th and the grunts, and that cheer echoes across America to this day. The NV A unit's losses were so heavy that the attack failed. Wilfong for a while was among the Cav's most decorated NCO's, when after four months at L.Z. Grant; Wilfong had two Silver Stars, three Bronze Stars and one Purple Heart.

On March 12th. the rising sun revealed 287 NV A bodies around L.Z. Grant's perimeter. Cold milk was flown in to refresh the soldiers, as the Cav's Cobra helicopters sprayed the NVA bodies, (after the 23rd, many "dead" had put up a fight). Command ordered Chinook helicopters to bring bulldozers to Grant to assist policing up the bodies. The smell was terrible, "You don't have too long, and we saw some very big holes the NVA had dug by the wire so we dumped them in there, and the dozer covered them over." said Jeffery Andrews. Those NVA, and another group buried in the dump, numbered 97 men, and they were excavated in 1994, after CBSs' 60 Minutes went to L.Z. Grant on a story called "The Spoils of War" with correspondent Steve Kroft. A few months later the Vietnamese Government dug them up, in a ceremonial process, complete with firecrackers and incense to honor the dead of both sides.

One March night, Command ordered a movie to be shown, "Planet of the Apes" was supposed to be a distraction for the men at L.Z.Grant, the movie was sparsely attended, because the soldiers did not want to leave their guns. The 77th was using up Howitzers at a rapid rate. The ideal pace of firing for a Howitzer was to fire ten rounds a minute for three minutes, then three a minute until cease fire. That rate was constantly being exceeded, and the 77th's cannoneers were receiving many new Howitzers. Capt. Capshaw took advantage of this and put an extra gun under tarps in case of emergency. There was a designated, "Hot Gun" ready for action at all times. The ferocious ground attack of March 11th was again stopped by "Stacked Deck". The 155's lost five men KIA, including their beloved medic, Roger Denny; from Mayna, Louisiana, the 155 Battery was split the next day with three guns sent to LZ Dolly.

Sappers

There was another sapper attack on May 12th, and again the GI's, this time "Wild Card" or C Co., narrowly escaped annihilation. This time the "Hot Gun" got a call from Echo's mortar men for illumination.

Preface

Immediate response showed 60 sappers were making their way inside the L.Z. There were already 32 on the berm, inside the wire, between the Infantry, and the Artillery, these sappers were dark and elusive, and there was a chaotic shoot-out across the L.Z. Echo's men helped "Wild Card" in killing the 28 NVA in the wire and soon enough, only two sappers were still alive. These POW's told of a Battalion of NVA who were waiting for the sapper's signal to charge L.Z. Grant and again, kill every American.

The 2/12th's A Co.s' Andrews and Hutchins, endured many days of contact, "Ace High" was whittled down many times. The line Companies would have to borrow a few soldiers here and there to stay operational. Then one day 13 of A's men were WIA under triple canopy jungle. The call was made for extraction, but the medevac could not land and the crew had to lower a "Stokes Basket" to the wounded men. A badly wounded GI was strapped into the basket, as the winch raised the basket, the NVA started shooting and either severed the cable, or the crew cut the cable, and the basket fell back to Earth, but 200 yards from A Company's men. A Company struggled for two hours to close the 200 yards to their friend. Presson recalls, "We were shooting so close to friendlies that all the 77th's crews were using the center gun, we never stopped." The GI said the NVA had been searching for him, and that the Artillery drove them back, upon reaching the L.Z., a lot of the Infantrymen walked over to the Artillery crews to thank them.

I traveled to Tishomingo, Oklahoma, on 20 June 2006, to see and meet Larry Hutchins. With me was my son Travis, and we picked up Arthur "Ace" Estrada of San Angelo, Texas. Art and I took Basic and AIT together in 1968, and he was with HQ Battery 77th thru 1969. We met with Hutchins, and his wife Ada Liz, we spoke of Vietnam for about an hour. "How I made my deros, I'll never know. I used to say, 'It was the Lord willing, and my momma's prayers, that got me home." said Hutchins. Travis told us how he was to start Boot Camp in August, at Ft. Benning, Georgia. It was quiet, so I looked at these old soldiers expressions; I saw admiration, and a little bit of envy.

When the time finally came to leave L.Z. Grant, the fellows at the Fire Direction Center figured out how to make a "Good Bye" salute. The 77th's Howitzers were aimed skyward, and each gun fired three rounds of illumination, "It looked pretty good" says Presson, "Good Bye, L.Z. Grant"... a six pointed star shown bright, and then faded out to black.

LZ Grant, 1969
Photo by Rick Kopec

The Living Ghosts

HOWARD FISHER

Del Mar to Vietnam, 50th Anniversary 1968-2018

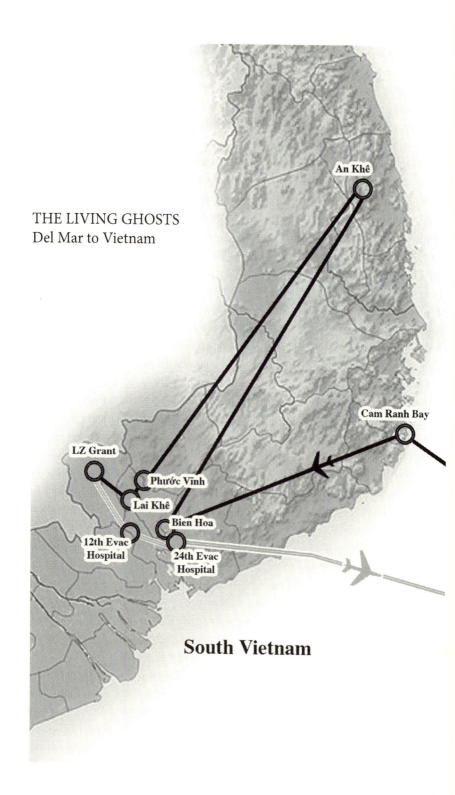

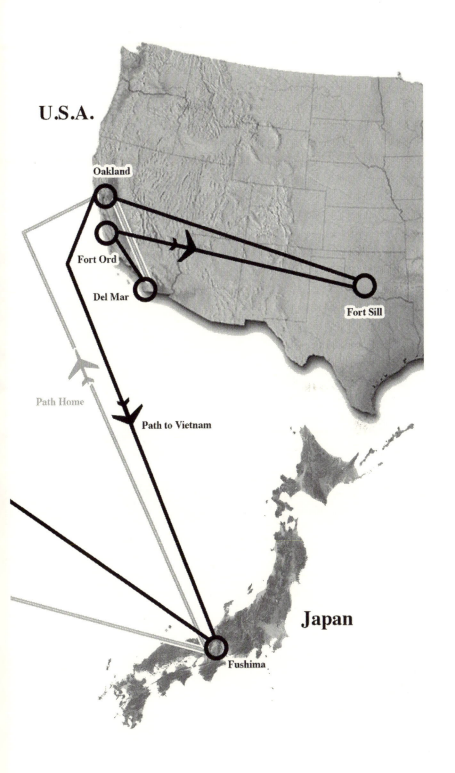

JUNE, 1968

THERE IT IS.

Jun 05, 2016 2:50pm

All soldiers fight, suffer, and die alone surrounded by friends... Pure allure... obscure to procure... and when achieved a voice asks, "Have you lived long enough? Do you want to go back"... Happy 4th ... H

Jun 11, 2015 5:45pm

The notice said... "...6AM, Oceanside bus depot, August 28th 1968..." My love for the Ranch, my people, my nation... Made it very hard to get to sleep, because tomorrow was about to come, still the drops from the coastal fog eased my mind, there it is...

Jun 18, 2017 5:26pm

Viet Nam flashback... Can still vision my teeth piling up on my palm and then a flood of blooded flesh and a helicopter landing close by and crawling

June, 1968 *There It Is*

into a stretcher and blood hitting the guy below me and he hides his face and when he peeks a look I flip him the bird and winds whip my drooly blood as the bird lurches up and the cool wind distracts me from watching the red hot landing zone blasting away...Fading away as the blackness takes over...H

Jun 21, 2017 8:30pm

July 1968... Sleeping on the beach next to the tres palms and I feel an icy cold only to awaken to see a big chunk of ice balanced on my hip and melting... about then Steve Gavin says... "Here" and hands me my draft notice... Greetings from the President... 6am August 28... Oceanside bus depot...H

JULY, 1968

TWO REALITIES.

Jul 03, 2016 8:09pm

I want to thank Uncle Sam for drafting me as I just earned a $30 check for talking about traumatic brain injuries so next week's breakfast will be on our Uncle... Plus they said my head was flawless, beautiful, marvelous...H

Jul 20, 2018 8:05am

Fifty years ago... Del Mar was easy living and I had it good, nagging me was that I might miss out on Viet Nam... That way I wouldn't be living on dead man's legs, all I needed was a scar.

Jul 20, 2017 2:59pm

Summer 69... Locked in an infection ward with screaming Marines for 79 days I anxiously awaited the moon walk, but... and this was huge... Hee

July, 1968 *Two Realities*

Haw was on at that hour so the Marines wanted to skip the Armstrong show live from the moon! Twas like yesterday... July 23rd right?...H

Jul 21, 2017 3:02pm

July 1968... Daydreaming again on the beach when it seemed I lurched fast forward and had just been shot in the mouth, or should I say imagined... About six months later, well two realities collided...H

Jul 25, 2017 2:51pm

She wanted my name but my dog tags were gone so she took scissors and cut off a boot because our names were inside the boots and after filling out my papers she said I was too far gone for the field hospital, so off to the 24th evacuation hospital near Saigon, where I sat with maybe 40 guys all with head wounds, I went last so it was a long slog of a night, February 23 ...1969...H

AUGUST, 1968

A DUCK IN A DOG'S KENNEL.

Aug 02, 2018 1:50am

Twas 50 years ago, 1968... The Del Mar ranch was quiet, every eucalyptus nut that hit the roof, every drop from foggy mists, hearing my father grind his teeth, all paths led to the Army... August 27 loomed like Moby Dick about to rage and kill... A baptism under fire in the land of Viet Nam or stay comfortable in my America... Oh boy... America love it or leave it, or both.

Aug 05, 2018 11:21am

Camp Pendleton's artillery keeps my PTSD in the here and now... The sound is like a HUGE purr with a mild shake... Like a Huey flying the area, making reflexive thoughts here fifty years on... Never watched MASH... Solitary man... peace peace peace.

August, 1968 *A Duck in a Dog's Kennel*

Aug 05, 2013 3:34pm

Memories from August... 1968... Sleeping on the beach, someone puts ice on my hip and I awaken to see a crowd of surfers, Steve Gavin is holding my draft notice, "August 28th, 6 a.m. at the Oceanside bus station, don't expect to return home"...H

Aug 09, 2017 2:10am

1968... Draft tomorrow... Jack London termed inheritance as ... "Living on dead man's legs" and since I had inherited land I figured it was time to earn it... I fitfully slept, I heard dad's teeth grinding, and the drops came from the Eucalyptus leaves and soon enough we were driving to Oceanside bus depot...H

Aug 13, 2013 2:00pm

August 27th, 6 am report to the Oceanside bus station...1968... America love it or leave it... Amnesty? Never mentioned in '68... I got nothing to say bad about the Vietcongs... but I own a chunk of land thats to die for, time to roll... See ya Pop... But sleep wouldn't come, and so I listened as the Ranch's moths were banging against the porch light, and heard the dew begin to drop from the Eucalyptus... Scared? Maybe...H

Aug 16, 2018 5:32am

1968.... Awaiting the draft... Languid days... Laying on the hot sand pulling the sand to my chest, and using the cool Pacific to escape, I wondered if I should try to be in better shape but agreed with myself that the Army would do it for me... The Del Mar life was an Eden, doves cooing and Uncle Bird smiling, the sandy loam of home turf, or where the turf meets the surf... to die for...H

The Living Ghosts

Aug 19, 2016 10:33am

August 28 ...1968...We'd raised our right hands and been sworn into the Army near sundown and now we were riding the bus to Fort Ord as full members of America's military... and the drill instructors licked their chops and drooled at the thought of all this fresh meat...Furtive sleep... LA to Ft. Ord...H

Aug 22, 2014 10:57am

27 Aug 68... After being sworn in we bused to Monterrey where we were met by screaming drill instructors in the middle of the night... I felt like a duck in a dog's kennel...H

Aug 22, 2018 2:54pm

1968... One week till USArmy... Big desire to do something big and like every 18 year old figuring my country, right or wrong... I looked at my military idols, Ernest Borgnine, Vic Morrow, Phil Silvers... and Gomer Pyle... They all were having the time of their lives but Viet Nam was taking 1,000 young lives of American soldiers a month at $10,000 a pop per life... No time to wonder why.

Aug 26, 2013 2:32pm

Draft day '68... "Hearing test machine is out" muttered a soldier, "Really" I said "NEXT" he replied... Then a Marine filled the doorway and yelled, "Every third man is going to the Marines!"... "Waitaminute, what, who's he talking to?" Said Art "Ace" Estrada...H

August, 1968   *A Duck in a Dog's Kennel*

Aug 26, 2018 8:27am

March 1973... Back in hospital for plastic surgery when the prisoners were brought back to America... Leaning out a second story window, I was above a milling throng and under hundreds of others leaning out of the six story San Diego Naval Hospital next to Balboa Park...John McCain was in one of the limousines that delivered them from Miramar... We yelled ourselves silly...H

Aug 27, 2013 9:01am

Thanks to all for Veterans salutations... Having cleaned 5 deer in the last week I'm tired, Vietnam scared my soul and at night I retreated to visions of Del Mar, my mind wandered the Town and waded the beaches... Love of Country...H

Aug 27, 2015 9:31am

Yesterday's "Wounded warrior" breakfast went bad for me... I sat with the director, and expressed dismay that there are still fresh wounded after the war ended in 2011, I also noted that in all my years as a wounded vet, I've personally never been asked by anyone or any group if I needed help, ooops!. With raised voice she said, "I run 6 houses for the wounded"... good for her but this culture may need to be scaled down so that our all volunteer Army can be properly cared for by the United States of America, not the public... Peace would be nice...H

Aug 27, 2012 6:14pm

I used to watch my grandfather (Distinguished Service Cross April 19, 1917) watering the dying orchard, peacefully content... I saw my dad gazing at horizons (USS Farragut, Aleutians and Tarawa{biggest debacle since Pearl Harbor})...I watched my Uncle scream at Eleanor Roosevelt and her link to the Kamikazes that never left him at peace... I went to Viet Nam hoping not to kill anyone, and left feeling unlovable, so I move over on the family bench for my son Travis hoping he too sees Peace in his post Iraq days... Happy Veterans Day to all ...H

Aug 27, 2014 8:53pm

3 Sept 68...1 week in and I feel like a professional janitor... We got uniforms and hair cuts but we still are not in boot camp, that's soon... Everywhere we go we hear others songs, "I wanna go to Vee Ett Naam, I wanna..."H

Aug 26, 2017 11:55am

September 1968 ... Two weeks into boot camp singing... "I want to go to Vee et Nam... I want to kill the Charlie Cong"... September 1969 ... Spent the month infected and dressed in white the 79 days after bone graft surgery... September 2017 war seems nostalgic as PTSD brings memories of being young and alert... Ken Burn's documentary on my mind...H

Aug 28, 2016 7:54pm

Boot camp at Ft. Ord is best remembered for dinner time ...with the sun on our backs we waited in a slow line smelling the chow and salivating over the chocolate milk machines that never ran out and the wholesome stacks of steaks and mounds of mashed potatoes, the cooks were fat and eating bread dipped in grease... September 1968...H

SEPTEMBER, 1968

BROKEN HAIL.

Sep 03, 2014 1:17pm

8 Sept 68... We sing, "I gotta girl in Kansas City..." as we run toward the rifle range... "She's got dimples on her titties, Honey oh Babe be mine" and so it goes with the 2nd week in our man's Army...H

Sep 08, 2014 4:09pm

18 Sept 68... Foods good... The run to the rifle range is in the thickest dust that thousands of boots have ever trod, until it is a tunnel of choking sand.. The coastal sage smells of home... a long time ago...H

Sep 14, 2015 5:07am

1968... "Eleven Bravo, Eleven Bravo" barked the drill instructor, but to me, he said "13 Alpha 10" and gave me the 1,000 yard stare, but then he smiled and muttered "artillery" and just like that I was spared the Infantry...

About 47 years ago, and still one of my favorites...Art Estrada got to hear the same...H

Sep 15, 2017 8:31pm

Ken Burn's documentary about Viet Nam had a man saying... "After being there a while I figured mankind in war shows our worst instincts, and life is just finishing school"...H

Sep 16, 2016 5:27pm

Sept 18 1968... It was the day for the gas chambers and the drill instructors had been talking it up for weeks about how we would be puking into the masks... My luck held true and I was on KP which meant working in the kitchen...I always have been lucky...H

Sep 18, 2014 12:27pm

Oct 68... One month in and stoked to be on KP... First I peeled a small hill of potatoes, then cranked up the stereo in the empty dining room and heard the song, "Fire!..I think you should burn"... earning my $99.50 a month...H

Sep 19, 2017 10:22am

Ken Burn's documentary is getting closer to my time in the war and scenes bring back the heat and fetid humid jungle smells plus the smell of artillery and Army gear and dust rising from the trembling earth as bombs shake us and we grind our teeth and watch the dust rise straight up with every bomb...H

September, 1968 *Broken Hail*

Sep 20, 2016 11:00am

Insomnia memories, there is a guy in Cardiff who tells a memory of hiding at night from the Viet Cong and unable to see even his own hand, and some one's hand grabs his boot and quickly lets go, it's a spooky memory, in training we hear of a line of enemy soldiers with no visible end to the bobbing heads passing a night defensive positions... Oh boot camp memories...H

Sep 20, 2017 10:03pm

Ken Burns documentary on Viet Nam covered from January to July 1968, with May 68 being the highest death toll of the war... Graduating that June from high school the War was like a huge vacuumed effect sweeping away the idle youth and offering an escape from hometowns across America for those seeking adventure, secure that millions of others were caught up in the biggest event of our times... Unbearable to fathom not going, and to earn the inheritance left me by mom, I shouldered up my share of the burden and set out to find out if my balls were big enough to handle it, a year later it was over for me, and I pulled hot sand up to my chest staring out at the sea's horizon, secure in Del Mar.

Sep 24, 2017 9:43pm

Ken Burns' showed three significant dates for me, the show mentioned August 29th as the Chicago convention's police rioted against the protesters, that was our first full day in the Army... then January 20th showed Nixon congratulating his team on the same day we landed in 1969... then the end of February when the second year of the offensive two kicked off and that night was February 23rd when I saw my teeth looking like broken hail as they pooled in my palm and I dumped them in the dirt there... where they still are about 25 miles North of Saigon...H

Sep 25, 2017 10:01pm

Ken Burns' documentary day 9... In March 73 I was back in the San Diego Naval Hospital briefly for an operation and I was there when the prisoners were returned and we cheered as the men were driven to the hospital in limos in a line from Miramar to the hospital doors where we raucously welcomed them in a joyous moment of American history and I was there...H

Sep 27, 2017 9:52pm

Ken Burns documentary for me was like a ten day date...I want more but mimicking the real deal, for me, the answers aren't there, like am I brave... was it just... Is freedom linked to War... Who's the real brave, the pacifist or the warrior? ... A melancholy conclusion is that every generation has its own Viet Nam, and the endless supply of the uninitiated bodes poorly toward peace...H

Sep 29, 2016 1:44am

The soldiers in boot camp included college graduates, average Joes and in general, not athletes, but good Americans amongst whom 58,000 were killed in Viet Nam while Donald played 3 sports in college and claimed to be unfit...Voting for him is spitting on the graves of my fellow soldiers...H

Sep 29, 2011 1:33pm

I'm low on ammo and thirsty as Hell, may never get to Heaven, and I've been to Hell.

Sep 29, 2017 3:04pm

1968... Fort Ord... October... Hospitalized until the hour of graduation I missed marching in the final ceremony, but out the window you could hear the boots slapping the pavement and then the drill... "One oh one" troops, "ONE oh ONE" ... "Patch on my shoulder"... "PATCH on my SHOULDER..." "Pick up your ruck, and follow me" "Pick up your ruck and follow me..." "Airborne Infantry"... "AIRBORNE INFANTRY"... I still get chills...H

Howard (Left) *"Discovered this action photo from boot camp on smear-ur-face-with-grease-and-go-get-gassed day... Well as luck would have it I was on KP."*

OCTOBER, 1968

HOLD YOUR BREATH.

Oct 01, 2014 10:53am

3 Oct 68... Nightly alone in a group of 40, one must learn tolerance in a hurry... The black guys sing a lot, so do the Latinos... "Sunshine, blue sky's, Please go away, my love has found another and gone away"...H

Oct 01, 2011 6:10pm

Gave a calendar to my friend John Baca... He sat next to Obama on the Midway on 11/11/11... Veterans day... I'm envious... John was wounded near L Z Grant... The same place as me in Vietnam, when on February 10th 1970 he earned The Medal Of Honor...

Oct 03, 2014 8:04pm

7 Oct 68... Half way thru boot camp... Nightly fogs smelled of the sea, and I'd be running on those sandy hills in my mind's eye, perhaps valuing it more now that it was so far away... from Ft. Ord...H

Oct 05, 2016 5:25am

1968... Boot camp was over and we gathered in winter coats to greet the sun as we were flown to Oklahoma's Fort Sill with its fat NCO's and snowy barracks filled with cannon fodder learning the basics of Artillery... Hurry up and wait...H

Oct 07, 2014 8:55pm

13 Oct 68... If the army told you where you were going you wouldn't go, but in boot camp the whole goal was to get out and not be re-cycled, Viet Nam rather than re-cycle... We all believed in the girl from 'Kansas City'..H

Oct 13, 2014 7:03pm

20 Jan 69... Deplaning I saw a bunch of old weary soldiers ready to go home and my first impression of Viet Nam was that it reminded me of chaotic Tijuana... The music was bizarre, like a series of accidental noises... get me a gun I say 'cause I'm a fightin' son of a bitch...H

Oct 18, 2017 2:45pm

October 1968...At the end of boot camp you feel like a god you see the new recruits and sing loud... "I gotta girl in Kansas City, Honey, Honey... I gotta girl in Kansas City, Babe, Babe...I gotta girl in Kansas City, she's got dimples on her titties..." It was timeless and so was the Army...H

Oct 23, 2017 2:29pm

1968... Boot camp over, about 150 in my class... Hold your breath... 78 go to the Infantry... 10 to cook... 10 get artillery, the rest are Regular Army and the "RA's" get specialties... The drill told me... "Fisher, 13 Alpha 10... uh artillery" and he smiled his white teeth grinning thru his black face, happy for my fate... Off to Fort Sill Oklahoma, then RVN...H

Oct 24, 2016 6:14am

Truth... Grandpa got the Distinguished Service Medal for WWI...Dad was in the Navy at Tarawa in WWII... All but 5 of my teeth still are in the soils of Viet Nam... Service tells you a lot about yourself and your fellow American at their best, I would do it all again and fuck Trump's draft dodging ass...H

NOVEMBER, 1968

HERE WE GO.

Nov 04, 2015 6:36pm

Happy Veterans Day... "Please remit, $96,202.90" that was in October of 09... No explanation, to this day... Representative Issa's office was of no help, and Hunter's office was (helpful), but I'm still waiting for WHY I owed the $$$$$, (that I never paid) so my pension was stopped for a year, before it all went away, with no explanation... FTA...H

Nov 06, 2015 5:09am

Like most Veterans, I wish my flesh and blood was spilled in the dirt of Viet Nam as toward the beginning of the end of human's obsession with War... No such luck... Happy Veterans Day...H

The Living Ghosts

Nov 08, 2017 2:32am

1968 ...becoming a veteran smelled like Army gear, the stacks of equipment or uniforms or even the chow halls all smelled down home and as American as apple pie, the food was way better than at home, (sorry dad) and working together formed a group that teamed up becoming effective and bonding into a mixed race of brothers, loyal to each other and with warm and fuzzy emotions, life was and still is good... When you march together and sing together and suffer together you grow together... I salute all veterans...H

Nov 10, 2017 5:19am

1968... Fort Sill Oklahoma... Snowy and too cold for a Californian, I was the jeep driver for our Company so I escaped a lot of suffering and nights would pass listening to soldiers singing, "Sunshine blue skies, please go away, my love has found another and gone away. With her from my future, my life is filled with gloom so day after day I stay locked up in my room, I know to you it might sound strange, but I wish it would rain rain rain..."...H

Nov 10, 2015 8:53pm

My first thought after getting shot... "So that what it feels like to be shot"...then came a voice, "Have you lived long enough?" Followed by "Do you want to go back?"... I can't explain it... nor forget...

Nov 11, 2016 2:28am

Was it lonely being in service? Well the artillery lectures were only survivable by daydreams...I watched the Monarchs massing on our eucalyptus grove and threw the nuts at our friends, it snowed once and in my mind we drove in it again to Black Mountain and got in a snowball battle on its barren dusty hills ...but after the day dream you were back in the Army dressed the color of a bunch of pickles.

November, 1968 *Here We Go*

Nov 11, 2015 6:22am

December 68... Most military jargon was of no great consequence... PVT or PFC.... even SP4... or red leg... but there was one that mattered... Fisher Howard... RVN...those 3 letters... those letters were to cost me a lot... nearly my life... RVN...H

Nov 11, 2016 7:06pm

December 1968 Fort Sill Oklahoma... So cold with snow and what had I got myself into... The Army was getting tense with a few fist fights and at night the soldiers sang soulful songs... "Sunshine blue skies please go away, My love has found another and gone away, With her from my future, my life is filled with gloom, so day after day I stay locked up in my room, I know to you it may sound strange...But I wish it would rain..."... On and on as each man tried it...H

Nov 11, 2013 8:08pm

1968... Flying home for Christmas leave, the Beatles white album in hand, the parties were all readied up, to open once there, ordered to Viet Nam we didn't care, hell we weren't in the Infantry so not to worry...Merry Christmas Past and Present...H

Nov 12, 2012 11:16am

Well like I say, its the time of the year where my mind wanders back to 1969 and the allelopathy of Viet Nam plants itself in my presence... to exorcise it I must write of it so beware all who read my stuff, here we go again... Mucho amor...H

Nov 14, 2017 6:03am

Fort Sill Oklahoma 1968... My paycheck was $99.60 monthly and it went into the pay phone slots, at twilight I trod one hundred yards in windy sleet which brought the relief of the phone booth, California would still be sunny and the waves were hot, but in the freezing phone booth you had to push quarters until it faded off to dark... Then you kicked snow back to the barracks ...H

Nov 14, 2011 2:18pm

3 weeks until Jesus' sister will appear, a living Goddess, and as such she will be all about healing the mess we are in, I'm sure she wants the end of War and she'll be for dismantling the industrial military complex... Heaven on Earth... Here we go...H

Nov 15, 2017 9:47pm

1968 Fort Sill Oklahoma... The daydream ended like the first one when a giant sting hit my mouth extending my soul to the limits and a little beyond, we had the rumors and the training was for Viet Nam so I figured it no big...H

Nov 29, 2017 7:03pm

1968... Homeward from Fort Sill and it's so cold in Oklahoma that we wear heavy winter issue in fact I still have the heavy overcoat because after two weeks in Hot California, I forgot it and left it in Del Mar... Huge party went well until Pat Medea and Katie Klies... The cops followed them to the bash and the rest is history...

Leaving the dancefloor, I saw a big Marine coming my way in the packed kitchen. "I hear you're the host" he said. We talked for a minute, "I've been at Camp Pendleton for four years, working on the loading docks, been to every party from Riverside to Imperial Beach looking for the fabled "California Party", after all that time I've found it" and he beamed from ear to ear...H

Howard outside his hooch on LZ Grant, Reading girly magazines "for the articles".

DECEMBER, 1968

NO ONE BELIEVED IN WAR.

Dec 04, 2015 12:48am

1968... Home on leave, we had a really big party going, and the bonfire was lit, when Katie Klies had the bad luck of the cops following her to the ranch house... The officers told me to go home, so I hid until the police gave up finding "the host"... and we got the party re-started... We go to Viet Nam in a few weeks, it was Time to party... January 20th was coming fast...H

Dec 05, 2011 9:38am

Today I mark... 62 revolutions around the Sun... Life is great... Now my job is to maintain a healthy body so no more snakebites, shrapnel, dog bites, barbed wire rips, broken arms from skateboarding... in other words... Yeah I'm old...H

Dec 12, 2016 8:38pm

1968 Fort Sill Oklahoma... Identical daydream from six months ago on the beach where I dozed... This time in the barracks trying to sleep and I felt steel rip my teeth from my jaw as my imagined wound flared my lips into bloody strips, and then I dreamed it all again and well... I knew it was significant of a hard time on my horizon... I dreamt of the ranch and the sandy earth that I would die for ...H

Dec 15, 2016 10:06pm

Sometimes PTSD is like a trail of breadcrumbs that you dropped going into the worst place you've ever been and yet you can't not follow because you need to survive so you see the blue sea then white sands and green jungle with red Earth and swoon...H

Dec 09, 2011 9:00am

43 years ago... 5 days into Viet Nam we get our M16s... Mine was old and battered and so I told the gunsmith... "Whats your specialty?" He said. "Artillery" I answered... "Don't worry about it" he waved me off. At that Time 1,000 GI's a month were being killed...H

Dec 19, 2017 2:05am

1968... Home on leave... 2weeks... Eucalyptus and cascading leaves, monarchs, but look what's coming... Typical hooch on LZ Grant.

December, 1968 *No One Believed in War*

Dec 21, 2013 7:01pm

1969... Dwelling back 45 years... Friends called us "Cannon fodder" and no one believed in the war but we were to go on the 20th so it was personal... I was the Captain's driver so I could stay out of the snow. Oklahoma sucked... Warning people... I'm going down memory lane again.. Best to avoid me for I get weird....H

Dec 22, 2016 6:56am

1968 home from the Army... Huge Bonfire and a rocking band with a packed house dancing to the white album until Katie Klies had the cops follow her out to the ranch... "Is this a bust officer?" She smiled..." Why yes it is, but this is a police raid".

Dec 23, 2016 8:41pm

Ft. Sill Oklahoma... 69... One week to go and snowy... and then Viet Nam.... So the cruel cold was soaked into our bones, and our vapid expressions were all we could muster, pale, and to me, the tropical heat sounded far away but promising... of change... and that we would get...H

Dec 26, 2015 6:54pm

1968... Thousands of painted ladies swirled, and flitted, to and fro, as the years end drew near... I watched Cotton tails run for cover in the graceful Eucalyptus grove that towered over the Ranch... I packed my bag and left, kissing the sandy earth... America, Love it or leave it, or get drafted, and ship out for foreign adventures...H

Dec 27, 2017 9:13pm

I knew a man in Viet Nam, and wanted to know his fate, he listens to Rush Limbah and spews hate hate hate, I tried to help him learn again, stuff to make him great, he said he was going to get a gun, that shooting people might be fun, that our Nation needed more like him, it's been ten years and so I learned to let him go...H

Dec 29, 2015 12:27am

January 69...Back in the barracks in Oklahoma, it was fine to see the guys... Those LA Dudes started singing, "Sunshine blue skies..." and with all that song's nuances it was the most sung ditty... we were happy... and 18 days... until the War, would kill the buzz...H

Dec 30, 2017 9:41pm

This man worked in Del Mar for the city, in fact we worked together for years before one day he asked me... "Where did you do your basic?" I told him I remembered him and he said... "Yeah... What I say?" Harold Inouye was from the Islands bra... "You say if "You don't listen to me your buddy is gonna die" and with teary eyes we hugged.

Home on the Ranch for Leave

JANUARY, 1969

I CAN SEE IT ALL.

Jan 03, 2014 7:29pm

'69...With boot camp over the Sargent's were telling us our Army assignments... Almost everyone was getting... "Eleven Bravo"... infantry... Sarge called "Fisher" and then I heard him say... "Thirteen alpha Twenty" ...wow who cares what it is, its not INFANTRY... He grabbed his face and said, "Artillery" and smiled at my good fortune...H

Jan 03, 2016 8:40pm

1969...Ft Sill Oklahoma, at this point if an instructor wasn't a Viet Nam vet we could care less what he said... At night we tried to get drunk on 3.5 beers but we found it to be true, its like they say, "The first 100 times you quit drinking are the hardest"...H

Jan 04, 2016 7:58pm

1969... Deep snow in Oklahoma... Put a bunch of alpha males in a barracks and fights do break out... One had a guy bite a chunk out of another soldier's thigh, well he won the fight, but was arrested for damaging government property...H

Jan 04, 2014 8:19pm

'69... Even Today, at night with my back to the fire, in my nimble mind I can hear the instructors who'd already been to the War, word's... Like the soft spoken one who prudently refrained from pulling his trigger as enemy soldiers trailed next to him...H

Jan 05, 2018 4:22am

Tonight on 60 minutes reported on brain injury and referred to a veterans study on severe head injuries... Asked a few years back, to participate, I agreed only to have the left over surgical clips still in my face, be a problem for the scanners and so I was disqualified, the influence of long term influences came apparent to me long ago as for instance, when in theaters, my laughs were often alone and dogs have always been, were my furry friends as calmness is paramount to my peace, I've been compensated ever since Vietnam so I shut the fuck up...H

Jan 05, 2013 8:19am

Viet Nam '69... It started with me sleeping on my side on the beach in front of the tres palms at Del Mar, a surfer put a ice cube on my hip and while it melted, I woke up and Steve Gavin handed me my draft notice... August 28th 1968... What?...H

January, 1969   *I Can See It All*

Jan 06, 2013 5:44am

VietNam 69...In LA, we were all 300 men lined up naked with doctors inspecting and poking when a huge Marine swung open the doors and bellowed, "Every third man goes to the Marines!"..." Who's he talking to, us?" said Art Estrada...H

Jan 06, 2016 6:06pm

1969... Drafted (voluntarily) in August, I saw a fellow at Ft Ord,(a classmate of mine, Tom Cope's, brother, Bill). We talked and I saw him at the big party during Christmas leave, he said he was gonna fly Huey's... Got a purple heart...Welcome home Bill...H

Jan 06, 2013 8:15pm

Viet Nam 69... Truth be told the Army's boot camp was similar to survival in any High School, look for some friends and try not to stand out, become the jeep driver was my best move, as the Officers always returned to base with me driving, cool...H

Jan 07, 2013 7:57am

Viet Nam...69...After 4 months, we knew the war was to be after Christmas leave, one of us never returned, we were a mix, college grads and unemployed teenagers mainly carried by pride of self and now friendships that ran deep, brothers...H

Jan 07, 2014 2:47pm

'69... Everybody would sign the falsetto... "Sunshine blue skies, please go away" my 69... In the barracks in the evening soldiers would sing the falsetto song that starts, "sunshine blue skies Please go away, my Love has found another, and gone away", and on and on as soldier after soldier would try it to the end....H

Jan 07, 2013 6:45pm

Viet Nam..69.. Even though we dressed like pickles it was abstract, the war... I had two daydreams of being shot in the mouth, but when they said January 20th we would be there, it came home and now all there was to do was to hurry up and wait...H

Jan 07, 2018 8:04pm

January 13 1969.... One week until Viet Nam... Divided nation, soldiers wary of our leaders and wondering if dying for this country is worth it, 10,000 dollars we get by dying for a cause almost no one believed in...We soldiers now represented the loyalty needed for national goals of freedom and liberty... Brother hood for our neighborhood... Too much to understand and next stop is Viet Nam...H

Jan 07, 2018 8:09pm

January 5... 1969... Back in the Army making my $99.60 a month we were being trained in self propelled artillery... We had attitude and if the instructors weren't Viet Nam veterans we didn't listen... In the Army if you knew where they were going to send you, it is said you wouldn't go... and we were going on the twentieth... to Viet Nam...H

Jan 08, 2013 8:12am

Viet Nam 69... All instructors were recently back, they began and ended their classes with personal stories, "We saw so many of them on the trail that we held fire and let them pass" type stuff, we were getting the idea that one man's Life was nada...H

Jan 08, 2016 4:27pm

1969... Short timers in Oklahoma, when the Army wants to bivouac in the snow... I was well established as the Captain's driver so I knew I'd be driving back to camp, to add to my pleasure I got a big package at mail call, (which the officers gobbled down whilst I drove)... ah well such is life, I cranked up the heat in the empty barracks... Slept like a log...H

Jan 08, 2013 6:59pm

Viet Nam 69... Singing "Next stop is Viet Nam" we learned the War's jargon and tried to rationalize, duty, country, honor, but we weren't natural killers, Danny Hackett sang Bob Dylan songs in marches, he also was a Florida University grad... soon KIA...H

Jan 09, 2013 7:41am

Viet Nam 69... We felt safe, being artillery (plus paid 99$ month)... 1,000 men a month, mostly infantry, were being killed in January 69... In the Army it is said that, "If the Army really showed you where you were going, you probably wouldn't go"...H

Jan 09, 2016 5:18pm

1969... 1 week from deployment and the Army decides to teach us self-propelled artillery... in the snow... There only in body, our minds were already overseas...H

Jan 09, 2013 6:22pm

Viet Nam 69... By night my soul flew back to Del Mar, quiet since the freeway opened, nearly deserted beaches from September till Summer, I ran the trails of the Ranch, swung in the trees and dreamed of its sandy lands... It was hard to be away...H

Jan 10, 2013 8:39am

Viet Nam 2013...Just received/read a letter from a fellow soldier who still fights the War every night, he woke up recently choking his wife and thought he was in 1969, on a day he killed... A less violent world is what we want, is it asking too much?...H

Jan 10, 2014 9:54am

'69...45 years since Viet Nam... A week to go until in country, and I became resolved to get thru this without killing anybody, should be a piece of cake 'cause I'm in artillery and therefore safe as a cat on Grandma's sofa...H

Jan 11, 2013 8:05am

Viet Nam...69... How to handle the War? Scam? Natch, keep eyes wide open for opportunities, avoid the jungle, no gung-ho stuff, lets hope to play a piano in a Saigon whorehouse, and join the peaceful revolution back home... Success...H

Jan 11, 2013 8:44am

Viet Nam...69 The Army decides to train us on mobile artillery but we don't pay attention, hell we never heard of it and I never saw any in Viet Nam, so it was the Army at its best, confusion and convictions all around...H

January, 1969   *I Can See It All*

Jan 12, 2013 7:05am

Viet Nam...69... A week from Today we get to "In Country"...to recap, 4 months of training brings me and Joe Cisneros and Art Estrada to the cusp of the War, we're heading to California to be outfitted with the Jungle uniforms so here's my suggestion to you, if you're coming, be lean, mean, and be a fighting machine, its gonna be bloody, and over at the end of February... So pick up your helmet and put it on... Let me know if you're saddling up with us...H

Jan 12, 2016 3:12pm

1969... I met a proud lady the other day who said she was among the 100 thousand Americans who marched in front of the pentagon in 1967... I missed 1968 what with high school and then the Army... 1969 we're 5 days from Viet Nam for America I guess..H

Jan 12, 2017 6:54pm

January 69 ...Travis Air Force Base California...I see a man say Psssst to Arthur Estrada and the two disappear for many hours and later Art says his brother wanted to take his place and serve his tour so to keep Art from Viet Nam and all its gore... an act of love that Art turns down and we get closer to departure a little scared by the whole event, what could be so bad and weren't we gonna work in a Saigon cat house?...H

Jan 13, 2014 7:47am

1/17/1969... O400hrs... Quiet in the barracks... "On your feet, be in formation with all your gear and ready to deploy, first, shit, shower and shave, and be outside in fifteen minutes"...you are going to Viet Nam..." Who's along with me this year?...H

Jan 13, 2013 8:16am

Viet Nam 69.. All soldiers are stoic appearing, but they are human and they dread the "Dear John" letters that we got, my girlfriend drove me nuts as she was late and the pay phone bulged with my quarters...H

Jan 14, 2013 8:20am

Viet Nam...69.. Its the Army's way, you hurry up and then you wait, Left Ft. Sill Oklahoma and we'll land at San Francisco so guys are phoning home and making secret plans and some soldier is chasing his brother to stop him from going...H

Jan 14, 2018 8:12pm

Howard Fisher1969... We slept most transports but Travis Air Force base outside of San Francisco was the stop/supply for the war and thousands of men were mixed up amongst massive piles of equipment that somehow smelled magnificent and to pass time soldiers were asleep all about the chaos like in a pile of boots or whatever, we spent a few days there and Arthur Estrada disappeared after his brother appeared amongst the gear and mysteriously took him away...H

Reply to this entry from Arthur Estrada:

"My brother Bob who had just returned from his tour of Vietnam with the 101st Air Borne Div. had tried to trade places with me, knowing what was about to happen to me and my comrades. Not being able to do that we went to S.F. for what could have been our last party together. On my return I was able to get my gear in a matter of hours instead of days and reunited with my guys heading for Nam. Brother Bob was right ,we were heading to Hell itself."

January, 1969 *I Can See It All*

Jan 15, 2017 6:39am

1969... This day never happened as we flew 17 hours and landed in Japan then on to Cam Rahn Bay... We saw the beautiful Ocean blue then the white waves and sand then red Earth and green jungle and the big shock was the blast of hot air as the Tropics humidity hit our faces and we faced the big mystery of being in the war zone...We sat on the tarmac and flew to near Saigon... and the 19th turned into the 20th... Arrival...H

Jan 15, 2013 8:47am

Viet Nam 69...From Frisco to Oakland Supply Army Depot, where in a maze of equipment we weary soldiers looked for places to sleep, a few days here and we go, then I saw a man call to Art, they needed to talk privately... huh......???...H

Jan 15, 2016 7:40pm

1969... Goodbye snowy Oklahoma, hello Travis AFB, California...We soldiers stumbled about, within mountains of varied gear. Suddenly Art Estrada's brother showed up, and he privately offered Art to serve his tour, in Art's place, and save Art from Viet Nam, he had just come back himself ...wow...H

Jan 16, 2013 8:07am

Viet Nam 69... Time to go, next up, Katoda Japan Base then we are told to stand by because they say we need winter Field Jackets (we ended up turning them in upon arrival in country)... expecting 17 hours in the plane, we needed Art for humor, but he was gone...H

Jan 16, 2013 9:26pm

Viet Nam 69...With seconds to spare, Art shows and somehow gets his gear and takes his familiar place alphabetically in line, "What's the big deal?" he says, "What are they gonna do send me to Viet Nam?" and we got on the bus to do exactly that...H

Jan 17, 2013 8:08am

Viet Nam 69...The War was huge in our imaginations, like a ogre we were flying towards, I'd heard about it since 5th grade... and the little boy playing soldier in me didn't want the gates of hell to close before I got a chance to visit...H

Jan 17, 2014 1:55pm

69... Stuck at Travis AFB as the Army's lone seamstress is tasked with putting our names on the cool jungle fatigues, hurry up and wait...Army style... You new guys, like Peggy well here comes Infantry for you poor schmucks...H

Jan 17, 2016 7:08pm

1969...Travis AFB dragged on... There was a milieu of soldiers, many deeply tanned, and only recently back from "their" war, they spoke in pure military jargon, and laughed at their military humor, they were, ahem, vets...H

Jan 17, 2013 7:26pm

Viet Nam 69... Long plane ride, I dreamt of our Ranch... Cotton tail rabbits playing with the coyotes, and the bevy of creatures all smiled, in the little rolling hills, that filled with fog nightly, and heated the days with welcome sunshine, why did I leave?...H

Jan 18, 2017 1:24am

As a foreigner in a strange land, Viet Nam looked and smelled and felt hotter and stinky-ears were hearing bizarreness in music that was crashing sounds of mayhem, people hiding from the sun and mama sans sweating as they cackle and try to scam the GI's in fact we got a beer and my script was snatched out of my hand by the owner who kept it all and uttered curse words like "Fook you GI"....H

Jan 18, 2013 8:15am

Viet Nam 69... Yakoda, Japan was a frozen delight, I touched the ground then got back in the plane... Somewhere we crossed the dateline and away we go, commercial jet with stewardesses...H

Jan 18, 2014 2:42pm

'69... Long plane ride with a stop in Japan tonight and then on to Viet Nam tomorrow, we are giddy as hell especially since two of us only have a few months to live, there in beautiful Viet Nam...Yet I fear no evil as we fly to the country of Death...H

Jan 18, 2016 7:23pm

1969... Twas icy, and pitch black, in the "Land of the Rising Sun", I touched the wet cement and returned to the plane as fast as I could. Tomorrow we will land, after blue ocean, turns to white surf, then green jungle... Hello Viet Nam...H

Jan 18, 2015 8:05pm

24 January 69... After three days milling amongst a mass of military men we get assigned to the Air Cav so tomorrow its good bye to this replacement center and hello to An Khe... up North...H

Jan 19, 2013 1:17am

Viet Nam 69... Leaving Japan's rising sun, I sat with Art and Joe Cisneros from Baldwin Hills, easy going, he loved to laugh, he was to be a friend for Life, unfortunately his funeral would be the biggest event of his life, next July, "The Summer Of Love"...H

Jan 19, 2017 5:40am

1969... Art and I were in the Cav and flying South... one noticed the endless bomb craters and beauty mixed together... we landed at Phouc Vihn with its sticky red earth and thick fetid smells and we spent the night knowing that tomorrow we go to battle grounds ...and wrestle those pesky inner demons...H

Jan 19, 2018 6:18am

January 19th 1969... Flying to Viet Nam out of San Francisco seventeen hours stopping in Japan... Joe Cisneros and Daniel Hackett would soon be dead and me and Art we're fated for the Air Cavalry and it's combat forces... It's the Army way, if you knew where you were going you wouldn't go.

Reply to this entry from Art Estrada:

Had we known we would be celebrating 50 years of Mexican residents. You would still have that million dollar smile and I would have been a better surfer.

Jan 19, 2013 7:48am

Viet Nam 69... Flying in over the Pacific, it was blue, white red then green, and first impression was that this place is beautiful... We landed at Cam Rahn Bay and sat under the plane until we took off for the 90th replacement center at Bien Hoa...H

Jan 19, 2018 2:29pm

After a giddy flight the stairs felt like the humidity alone could kill, the air was thick with smells and we were soon in traffic next to jets armed to the teeth waiting to launch next to the airport's road, the Vietnamese looked through us and the chaos what we saw was remind-full of Tijuana... Dirty and dank smelling of tropical excess.

Jan 19, 2016 6:44pm

1969... 1st day's impressions...Viet Nam smells like a fishy toilet, with chaotic streets filled with ramshackle buildings and millions of little kids, mixed up with livestock and scooters scooting...H

Jan 19, 2014 7:41pm

69... Days pass in a milling mass of military men, endlessly checking to see if our names are listed to go to our new units.. Suddenly Jose B. Cisneros is gone to the 196th Light Infantry after being here for many months, poof... Gone...H

Jan 20, 2013 7:48am

Viet Nam 69...Lets review, less than 20 years since Korea, the lesson of never get involved in a land war in Asia is forgotten, sans strategic assets

Viet Nam is turned into W.A.R.R.(Weapons and Armies Research and Refinement or War for short)...H

Jan 20, 2013 11:40am

Viet Nam 69... Deplaning at Bien Hoa's 90th Replacement Center we passed the soldiers who were going home on the "Freedom Bird" I remember their faces and now I know they reflected "Kill anything that moves" but at the Time, it was scary...H

Jan 20, 2015 3:04pm

45 years ago tonight,19 Jan 69... In transit to Viet Nam, would the mountain lion eat the coyote? We were young and soldiers and we were sure it would be handleable, besides it was up to us to return safe... and lady luck...H

Jan 20, 2016 3:04pm

1969... Day 2... A soldier's personal goal is to survive the rumors and get to a good unit... We were told to avoid the Americal Division, Jose Cisneros went there and by his tour's half way mark he was in a shiny metal coffin, and the Army wanted the coffin back...H

Jan 21, 2018 2:12am

January 21 1969... Bien Hoa hosts the replacement center where we join a milling mass of soldiers who constantly scan lists of assignments hoping to not go to the Americal Division (My Lai)... to pass some time we go to a beer bar where I promptly lose my script to a man who snatched it all and disappeared as fast as a Vietnamese cat could go... Welcome to Viet Nam now watch your ass...H

Jan 21, 2016 6:56am

1969... Art and I leave the 90th Replacement center, and head into Viet Nam's military airports, which are full of men moving about. Some I saw were in handcuffs, and civilian clothing, at the end of the day we're in An Khe, the home of the First Cav... Ah...H

Jan 21, 2013 8:14am

Viet Nam 69... Assigned to the Cav we headed to An Khe, up North, so transports in Military airports, and I remember seeing more than one GI in handcuffs and being escorted back to their units by burly guards, huh?...H

Jan 21, 2014 7:07pm

'69... Air Cav... At An Khe, so Art Estrada and I go to many airports in transit, my main memory is of often seeing soldiers in cities under arrest, maybe more to learn? Viet Nam seems very 3rd World and the music is nuts...H

Jan 22, 2013 8:04am

Viet Nam 69...Assigned to the Cav, ubiquitous hueys brought the sounds to us, there was a constant rumble from artillery ala WWI, mixed with the helicopters, to form a calliope, plus Vietnamese music sounds like a drunken crazy mix..... The Orient...H

Jan 22, 2016 11:58am

1969...Flying over this beautiful land one sees endless bomb craters. The women are beautiful. An Khe is a mix of a Viet Nam hamlet, and a military Division Headquarters, oh yeah and the nation's music is so bizarre, like noise, with drumming and cymbals...H

Jan 22, 2013 7:09pm

Viet Nam 69... Being an incurable eavesdropper I'm hearing bizarre things, "I popped smoke and Charlie di-di-ed and the Cobras lit 'em up"... or how about all the Bible sellers that swarm us after dinner, selling huge expensive Bibles to send home...H

Jan 22, 2015 9:19pm

25 Jan 69...Viet Nam's lexicon was my focus by day 5 in country... For instance, I was using the urinal looking out the screen when I watched a jeep skitter to a stop... "I just shot an Arvin who tried to steal my jeep" so I knew he just shot a South Vietnamese soldier, and I said "way to go"...H

Jan 23, 2013 8:57am

Viet Nam...69, Art and I continue to take varied combat classes, rumors are that the local "girls" all have "Super Clap" that will earn you a place on some Island in the South China Sea, so infectious you'll never be allowed to go home... Yikes...H

Jan 23, 2014 11:47am

69...This era's memories are like my galley slaves, this group is usually easy to ignore but this time of year they clamor for air and say, "Hey old man use me or lose me" and so its been since leaving Viet Nam...H

Jan 23, 2016 3:44pm

1969... Walking to another class at An Khe when some GI says hey check out my apartment.. Electricity, and an 8 track stereo, he played Hendrix' "Are You Experienced" I decided I was not, not yet... It all seemed so otherworldly er foreign...H

Jan 23, 2013 6:01pm

Viet Nam69... The Cav's training center is vast and we hike everywhere, most of us have too much weight but the heavy guys are lagging and flagging, so I'm glad to be rail thin and the skinny little Vietnamese Papa Sans seemingly are stronger than us all...H

Jan 24, 2016 6:55am

1969... By now Americans have concluded that there's nothing strategic about Viet Nam, and at a cost of 1,000 soldiers a month, the war is getting old, on the ground it's survive 365 and escape...H

Jan 24, 2013 3:32pm

Viet Nam 69... Stuck in An Khe, or anywhere in the Army, you really need a buddy, my friend Art Estrada, could put a Buster Keaton deadpan on top of any observation, and relieve the tension, this quality was much appreciated as a bitching Army is a happy Army...H

Jan 24, 2013 6:38pm

Viet Nam 69...I finally get my M16, its ancient and battered and doesn't shoot straight... The gunsmith says "Don't worry about it" apparently he is a believer that artillerymen are as safe as the cat on grandma's sofa...H

Jan 25, 2016 7:09am

1969... Finally got my M16... What a let down it is so battered, the sights won't even line up! Its cracked and faded and appears to be quite aged, but it shoots... So soldier on... If the Army told you where you were going, you'd probably not go...H

Jan 25, 2013 8:09am

Viet Nam 69... In the middle of the night I ponder the question, "Thou shalt not Kill" and the loss of my personal innocence, taking Life was never my thing, and would I be lovable afterwards? Between the War and my future stood this year...H

Jan 25, 2012 1:22pm

VietNam '69... Booby trap class, I happen to sit behind 3 soldiers transferring into the Cav from the Americal Division... With hushed voices they were living ghosts and whenever another trap snapped off, they said, "There it is"... spooks...H

Jan 25, 2014 2:59pm

69... Here a week, training with the Cav, lunch yesterday with Montanyards and wow are they small and primitive looking, we get our m-16s tomorrow and with the constant rumble of the war in the distance, its a good thing...H

Jan 25, 2015 6:01pm

27 Jan 69...When issued my M16, it was a letdown, the poor old weapon was nearing the end of it's useful days indeed I was sure it was the oldest one still in use and then the gunsmith tossed it back unfixed when I told him I was in the Artillery... "Don't worry about it" he said...H

Jan 26, 2013 1:52am

Viet Nam 69...There's no doubt that being in a War zone makes one's senses come to full activation, eyes, ears, ect... PTSD memories thus seem explainable to me, you felt great, and want to be proud, so you become nostalgic toward yourself, Howard...H

Jan 26, 2012 8:33am

VietNam 69... Trudging up a hill in a long line of soldiers, I see a young Vietnamese girl approaching me, she steps to the side and pulls up her skirt, squats and pees, me being American, this is new, I'd seen a horse pee on a rock... Unforgettable...H

Jan 26, 2013 3:35pm

Viet Nam...69 My dreams of the Ranch are so strong that I see it even when my eyes are open, the coastal flana, the sea breeze, pinion nuts from the Pines, the ambiance of "the sticks" it all amounts to Paradise or as we know it... Del Mar, California...H

Jan 26, 2016 4:47pm

1969... Booby trap class... I saw 3 living ghosts, transfers from another Division, they whispered, hallow eyed, slack lips, pre-dead by all appearances, not a role model for survival in Viet Nam...H

Jan 26, 2014 6:52pm

69...Issued a battered M16... Looks sun burnt and ancient, the veteran of many tours and it barely shoots and only has sights that are stuck but the gunsmith simply asks me, '"Whats your MOS?" and when I answer Artillery he waves me off..H

Jan 27, 2012 8:13am

VietNam 69... In country training almost done... The Tower must be faced, I look up and up and someone grabs me and forcibly connects me to the cargo rope ladder and up I go... with ropes surrounding "big Jim and the twins", I'm forced off into space...H

The Living Ghosts

Jan 27, 2013 8:24am

Viet Nam 69...Figuring to eavesdrop on three transfers from the Americal (My Lai 68) I sit behind them in a bleachers, as we watch enemy sappers demonstrate how to waltz thru barbed wire, I listen to the three ghosts whispering for evermore...H

Jan 27, 2016 11:36am

1969... In all my innocence I saw the tower that stood in my way at An Khe, grabbed by my shirt, I automatically climbed up this huge monster tower, only to have a rope put next to the family jewels, I rappelled/fell ...after this day Viet Nam should be cake...H

Jan 27, 2015 3:39pm

28 Jan 69... In Viet Nam my own self-image was of an innocent, but some housewife had led me from virgin territory and stealing TNT in Jr High took some gloss off, but Viet Nam was just foul even for a hillbilly from Del Mar...H

Jan 27, 2014 6:09pm

69... Transferring soldiers into the Cav were burned out... I eavesdropped on three of them and the men were vapid and beaten down by something that was unspeakable... They were like living ghosts....H

Jan 28, 2013 8:27am

Viet Nam 69... Almost done in country training... but I see a Tower and as I look up and up and up someone slams me into the net ropes and says... "Get to the top, NOW" so I go and from up there you can see forever, but don't look down...H

Jan 28, 2012 10:46am

VietNam 69... Trainings over, assigned to 77th Artillery with Art Estrada, Art and I have stood next to each other since August 27th '68 and here it is January 29th '69... I know everything about him and he, me... At the last desk, we get split... I go on alone...H

Jan 28, 2015 8:44pm

1FEB 69... ITS time you earn your 99 bucks a month and report to the 77th Artillery near Cambodia a place swarming with the enemy that is making it tough to the tune of 1,000 average American's lives a month...H

Jan 29, 2013 3:47am

Viet Nam 69... I don't know how the Army works but somehow we both got assigned to C Battery 77th Artillery and with our new Cav shoulder patches I remember being quite happy as we headed back South, it'll take a few days to get to LZ Grant...H

Jan 29, 2014 6:37am

69... An Khe is becoming home... One soldier shows Art and I his billet and he's got a refrigerator and an 8 track player... I've seen the jungle, too much shrapnel, I'll stay here rather than go but alas they say to head South to the 77th Artillery...H

Jan 29, 2012 8:56am

VietNam 69... Flying to Landing Zone Grant(LZ Grant)... mesmerizing greenery dotted with bomb craters... LZ Grant looked like a scar on the jungle... I saw my new home as a dusty mass of men and equipment... The chopper landed "There it is" I said...H

Jan 29, 2014 6:25pm

69... Flying South we see a red dust filled world, hotter than hell, bombed until its looks over done, we get to the Cav riding a menagerie of aircraft... Tomorrow we'll get to the actual unit. At this Time in Viet Nam we were losing 1,000 Americans a month...H

Jan 29, 2013 6:31pm

Viet Nam 69...The sticky red earth has spread thru out our gear, I must say what a beautiful place this is, and pretty girls aplenty, the first one I closed on, saw me coming and quickly squat-pissed alongside the trail we met on... Unforgettable..H

Jan 30, 2013 5:19am

Viet Nam 69... We did boot camp, all the way to the last desk, then the Army separated me and Art and I flew away from Lai Kai alone for the first Time in this experience, in a Huey that leapt up into the air... Lemming to cliff... Airborne...H

Jan 30, 2012 10:01am

VietNam 69... Assigned to howitzer #5 with Presson, Jones, and Bernard... (I do this from Jan. 20th to Feb.23)... we didn't know this ground was soon to run red with blood, forever studied in the Army War College among the worst of '69... LZ Grant...H

Jan 30, 2018 11:59am

1969... Tenth day... Air Cav and Phouc Vihn with its red earth and mosquito nets host us amidst lots of aircraft sounds indeed, helicopters seem to never not crowd the sky... Tomorrow we check in the headquarters in

January, 1969 *I Can See It All*

Lai Kei... I never felt so alone, a lamb in the field, really thick air with the tropical rotten vegetation in Oriental mystery and the Vietnamese music is crashing bashing crescendo after another....H

Jan 30, 2016 1:53pm

1969... LZ Grant... Kool Aid in Orange flavor is the daily grog... The lack of fresh food means we eat rations that resemble that good old actual Army chow, one searches the kit for goodies, we also get one beer, Pabst Blue Ribbon... and one soda, Coke... Life is noisy...H

Jan 30, 2016 1:53pm

1969...Sunset, after chow the massive bible sellers would prop up their wares to ease the anguish of the replacement soldiers, "You want them to have this to remember you by" was the sales pitch...$$$...H

Jan 30, 2014 4:59pm

'69... Art and I report in to the 77th Headquarters...10 minutes later I am in a chopper on my way to my unit and for the first Time since induction, Art Estrada is not at my side, then I see a cancer sore in the jungle and we land at L.Z. Grant...H

Jan 30, 2013 6:39pm

Viet Nam 69... Humans see 110 million bits of data per second of which our mind tracks about 44 and we are aware of maybe 15...Flying into LZ Grant my memory was apparently on photograph for I can still see it all, bomb patterns everywhere...H

Jan 31, 2012 8:31am

VietNam 69... Artillery is a lot of work, adjusting "BOOOM" to the noise (BOOM) made me plug my ears (BOOOM) 155mm and 105mm cannons all day (BOOM) and all night, if it wasn't us, (BOOM) then we filled sandbags (BOOM) for the bunker (BOOOM)...H

Jan 31, 2017 4:35am

The 77th Artillery was headquartered in Lai Kai and we reported in to register and the clerk had a string on his finger for advancing the typewriter's space bar and Arthur Estrada knew repair so he asked about it and the clerk separated us for the first time since August 28th and so I got inside a Huey helicopter alone for the first time in the army and my friend Art was out of sight but not out of my mind...We flew to Landing Zone Grant, a slash clearance in the jungle that looked like a cancer waiting for victims seeking victory...H

Jan 31, 2014 9:06am

69...1st day on Landing Zone Grant... I seem to be popular, but its really the photo of my girlfriend thats so interesting that soldiers are gathering, when asked about her boobs, I say "Perky" and the crowd went wild...H

Jan 31, 2013 2:12pm

Viet Nam...69...Woke up on LZ Grant, its flat, to the West I see the Black Virgin Mt., we are in a clearing on top of a road that is closed, there are 300 men and swarms of helicopters that together form a frenetic scene as we fill sandbags and prepare to be bait for the local VC and the NVA forces that own the area, my hootch is a concrete half-pipe and my job is as a crewman on the 105 howitzer, there's 12 big guns and they fire intermittently day and night... The guys demanded to see my girl's photo, and she was so fine that the guys got pissed...H

FEBRUARY, 1969

THEY OWNED THE NIGHT.

Feb 01, 2017 12:25am

LZ Grant 69... Twilight we got beer, a Pabst Blue Ribbon cool but never cold, so unrefreshing that I usually traded for a soda... and looking around, there wasn't shit, no town, no people, no houses, nothing to die for at all, just an old French fort's foundation next to the road which we were blocking as the artillery rocked our world the concussion pushing us by the salvos of One Five Fives and our own One 0 Fives over over over and again BOOM...H

Feb 01, 2013 8:38am

Viet Nam69... Sleeping on LZ Grant would be possible except theres a war on, so I kinda dream, of sleeping, while listening to the radio calling missions, and being lifted up by the concussions of the big 155s, boots on, hungry, "there it is", say the vets...H

Feb 01, 2012 9:05am

VietNam 69... The philosopher Samuel Johnson, "Many men who skip the Army think meanly of themselves" I say "Soldiers who have been at war worry that they now are unlovable, and their Sins unforgettable, as well as unforgivable"...H

Feb 01, 2014 4:04pm

69... In 1994 when 60 minutes visited LZ Grant, it was a manioc farm, in 69 I saw nothing at all but scrubby jungle, nothing worth all the blood and books that continue to follow, I dreamt of Del Mar nightly, and ran the trails of the Ranch...H

Feb 01, 2015 7:32pm

2 Feb 69... Today's Viet Nam airports were a chaotic milieu. The masses of military were upstaged by the soldiers I saw in handcuffs, why? I'll never know but they were resigned and very sullen...H

Feb 01, 2013 8:15pm

Viet Nam 69... The pecking order in the Army can be a bitch, there's rank, unit, uniform, jargon, weapon, intelligence, home state, time in country, lifer or draftee, military specialty, personality, race or even me the "FNG" or fucking-new-guy...H

Feb 02, 2013 8:04am

Viet Nam... 69... Books about LZ Grant speak of the confluence of streams, and trails. CBS' 60 Minutes show from there in 1994 showed a farm... in 1969, 25 ft tall jungle surrounded the LZ, filled with little men

February, 1969 *They Owned the Night*

in black pajamas, with AK-47s, scrambling around... but only at night, we owned the day, they owned the night...H

Feb 02, 2012 8:33am

VietNam 69... Our radio barks, "Ducks on the pond" (visible enemy soldiers) "Gun 5 azimuth..." We shoot as fast as possible... 16 enemy KIA... We're stoked... That afternoon the Army sends us an extra can of Pabst Blue Ribbon each as our reward...H

Feb 02, 2014 6:08pm

69... Through closed eyes, one sees the red glare then the concussion lifts you from sleep as the BOOM rocks your rack, good thing the pays so good or this might not pay off... LZ Grant's lack of sleep was hard on this young man, I coulda' killed for it...H

Feb 02, 2015 6:29pm

4 Feb 69... Arrived LZ Grant...At this Time I lived with a crew and worked with 300 men in the jungle with nothing worth a damn nearby or within our vista...Whats to even fight over? Give me Del Mar in September...H

Feb 02, 2016 6:50pm

1969... Guard duty was quiet time on LZ Grant, I remembered the Ranch' hop-a-long cottontails, and the cooing doves, running on sandy grounds, and the heat of the California sun, it all seemed so very far away, an obtainable goal, after getting outta this place...H

The Living Ghosts

Feb 02, 2013 7:57pm

Viet Nam 69.... One night on guard duty (listen to radio for missions) I heard, "Somebody should shoot her"... "Fuck you, you shoot her" apparently a woman strolled up to the road block, turned, and walked away... Good Americans...H

Feb 03, 2012 8:41am

VietNam 69... Deep sleep is impossible (BOOM)... I'm so homesick I ache, I know if I ever get back to the Ranch, I'll kiss the ground and never leave... To sleep, I pretend to be at Flippi's Pizza in San Diego's little Italy, guy flips a pizza and zzzz...H

Feb 03, 2017 6:36pm

LZ Grant 69... Daytime was grape Kool Aid... with some orange... but K-rations kept the peace, you could trade parts and hope to get some peaches or the ultimate pound cake and two cigarettes... but the nights were long with radio watch where big Jim and the twins would remember home and the one you left alone... What was she doing now?...H

Feb 03, 2013 8:08pm

Viet Nam...The sun rises over a featureless plain, we spend the day blasting down the biggest trees with our artillery, the vets say its a sign we ain't going anywhere, the ruins of a French fort seem to be a warning, but we are bait, bait doesn't get to bail...H

Feb 04, 2016 1:23am

1969... Guard duty was Time for dreaming of California, remembering my Ranch with its hop a long cottontails, and cooing doves. I'd pretend to be running on the sandy trails, but first thing is, we gotta get out of this place...H

Feb 04, 2016 1:27am

1969... Today I received 33 pages of official reports about LZ Grant, forwarded to me by Captain Capshaw, my captain in the war... I was relieved to read that there were no casualties in my unit the night I was wounded, (still my teeth are still there, just sayin')...H

Feb 04, 2012 8:21am

VietNam 69... Mid morning lull so we hold a class, sitting in a circle on sandbags when shrapnel comes out of no-where, whapping the sandbag next to me, a chunk of steel 2 inches long and an inch wide, hot and nasty... "There it is" we say in unison...H

Feb 04, 2013 9:44am

Viet Nam 69... In the area of LZ Grant infantry were hurt by bullets, shrapnel, snakebites, "accidental" discharges, booby traps, pungi stakes, heat stroke, malaria, man goes berserk, bamboo cuts, and we Artillery were as safe as that "cat on grandma's sofa"...H

Feb 04, 2014 9:52am

69... Mornings come too soon after sleepless nights, the most important thing is what flavor is today's Kool Aid, Artillery is shoot and work with thick air that chokes you all day, it's hot and sunny and no time for bullshit... In other words, LZ Grant sucks...H

Feb 04, 2015 1:48pm

16 Feb 69...Historically speaking, America will soon have a man WALK on the moon,.. and in one more week from today, I trade LZ Grant for a cushy hospital gig...H

Feb 04, 2013 6:47pm

Viet Nam 69... Endless missions became rote, when we heard, "Gun 5! Ducks on the pond!" A well directed shot of White Phosphorous and 16 enemy were gone... This earned us our own Pabst Blue Ribbon after the sun set... I mean beer...H

Feb 04, 2016 8:36pm

1969... Reading the battle reports was eye opening as I learned the fate of a man with 6 months in his Army captured at LZ Grant, the fact that he was my enemy seemed silly, hell we could commiserate as they say, "A happy Army is a bitching Army"... Thanks again Captain Capshaw,,,H

Feb 05, 2012 11:52am

Julian Today...I take my son to the Wounded Warrior Breakfast... One legless Marine rolls up to me to shake my hand with his wife behind him, "good thing your face wasn't hurt" I tell the handsome man "Hey thats my money maker" he said...H

Feb 05, 2012 11:59am

VietNam 69... LZGrant is at a confluence of trails and waterways... We're killing a lot of enemy and the grunts are finding huge caches of materials... We know we should move... We don't know they're digging under us, and watching everything...H

February, 1969 *They Owned the Night*

Feb 05, 2013 3:12pm

Viet Nam 69... At times the dust would begin to spurt upwards, and the whole Earth would shiver, then once we were all bouncing and the vets said "Ark Light" and we knew it was the B52's laying out a 500 yard wide mile of death with 500 lb bombs...H

Feb 05, 2017 7:44pm

LZ Grant 69... Legions of mothers awaken when their boy dies overseas... My two premonitions were solid messages that I would be struck in the mouth and like a blowing wind it came and left me wiser, but on LZ Grant there was nowhere to go and the B-52s bomb closer every day... At least mom was already dead...H

Feb 05, 2014 8:21pm

69... 3 enemy soldiers stood up about 100yds in front of the LZ... We counted down from 10 on the radio then sent those men a flyin... 5 minutes later they were gone when the Infantry went to check the bodies... eerie to see...H

Feb 06, 2012 8:56am

VietNam 69... Everything is shaking "Arc Light" say the veterans... We look like bobble-heads and dust rises across the LZ... B-52s dropping 500 pound bombs as close to us as possible... Shaking like hula dancers we were in awe...H

Feb 06, 2014 9:01am

69... Dusk brought one soda and one beer for each soldier, warm but welcome it was Pabst Blue Ribbon... The evenings were cool and the armed forces radios were turned up playing.. "We Gotta Get Outa This Place"... yeah now you're talkin'...H

Feb 06, 2013 11:39am

Viet Nam 69... All spare Time, we work on our bunker, recently captured NVA soldiers say they have 120mm mortars, and thousands of men, in the tunnels safe, because they are deep and close to us...Oh really? We've been here too long already...H

Feb 06, 2017 2:31pm

LZ Grant 69... Shaking grounds make the dust wiggle as it rises... it's the B52s bombing... The full moon brings this observation... 2 weeks till no moon and that'll be time to be attacked, I climbed up on a bunker to see the jungle "You'd make a good target for a sniper" said Sgt Rabb with his tired old black face, weary bloodshot eyes staring awash...H

Feb 06, 2013 7:20pm

Viet Nam 69... LZ Grant's weaknesses were the unknown. In 1994, when asked by CBS' Steven Croft to explain the enormous loss of life at Grant, the NVA General grimaced and said the LZ was "Unacceptable, it had to be eliminated" the program called it "among the biggest combat stories of 1969, and then soon forgotten"...H

Feb 06, 2014 8:03pm

69... We shake like dolls as the B52's drop their payloads closer every day, dust rises straight up like a thousand snakes charmed out of the earth... oh yeah our fathers said after WW11, "Don't get in a land War in Asia"... ooops...H

February, 1969   *They Owned the Night*

Feb 07, 2012 8:14am

VietNam 69... In the middle of the night you could think... Ma died in 66 and passed us the Ranch East of Del Mar... It would be anathema for her to see me here trying to prove I'm worth it... I run the trails in my mind, barefoot with my dogs...H

Feb 07, 2013 2:02pm

Viet Nam 69... I close my ears as often as possible to protect them from the noise of the artillery, now Today 2013 I can still hear the muffled sounds of the snows piling up around me, and I heard my dog fart twice, so I did well back in LZ Grant...H

Feb 07, 2016 8:29pm

1969... The whole base would shake from the bombings... At this time in life I'd say a 6.3 earthquake rattling everything with no sound and no visual on the actual planes..... LZ Grant...H

Feb 07, 2014 8:39pm

69... It's said there's no atheists in fox holes... I always look for dogs for my comfort in Life's troubles to teach me about friendship and Life and Death, after LZ Grant I have never again been without "Man's best Friend"...H

Feb 08, 2018 1:43am

1969... LZ Grant... The 77th and the 30th field artillery were famous for operation Pegasus where they relieved the siege at Khe Shan and the veterans remarked on the similarities, outnumbered but dominant we had all the advantages of jets and helicopters but they came out of the ground like some ants determined to kill us all for their Uncle Ho... There was no where to go and running thru the jungle was hopeless, it was to be, do or die...H

Feb 08, 2012 8:25am

VietNam 69... Middle of the night on radio watch, first voice, "Someone ought'a shoot her" second voice, "Fuck you... you shoot her" I listened for a long Time... No-one shot, she walked up to the outpost turned and returned to the jungle...H

Feb 08, 2016 6:07pm

1969... Weeks on LZ Grant led one to a weary haze where sleep was a tonic to incessant noise, and concussive booms lifted one's feet off the ground day and night... A hell on Earth's heaven..H

Feb 08, 2014 6:49pm

69...We began to hear dogfaces say, "We gotta didi, no shit they ain't comming and with beau coup NVA here, we gonna run thru the jungle"... translation... We are camped on top of a North Vietnamese anthill and they are gonna swarm...H

Feb 08, 2013 11:09am

Viet Nam 69...Army brass has us issued "Co-fram" a new ammo designed to be better than the "beehive" that we know and rely on... Now if only we were trained to use this new stuff, because it seems we will soon need it... Alas, they forgot to train us...H

February, 1969 *They Owned the Night*

Feb 08, 2013 7:32pm

Viet Nam 69... The infantry found large caches of material and rice in 50lb bags daily, at dusk some would join us and tell about how they were sure we would be hit as soon as the moon came, they gave us some banners they found and although we didn't know what those banners said in Vietnamese, we shot them to nada...H

Feb 09, 2012 8:54am

VietNam 69... One of my biggest hopes was to not kill anyone and failing that, to not see anyone die... Noon, 3 enemy stand 150 yds away, looking at a clipboard, we start a countdown from 10... Two...One... KaBoom... Three souls... BOOM... Gone...H

Feb 09, 2013 10:44am

Viet Nam 69... LZ Grant had a swimming hole at the river, John Baca (my friend here in Julian) cut his hand badly diving in the water there, he also earned our nation's top award for heroism, the Medal of Honor on February 10th, 1970, by LZ Grant...H

Feb 09, 2018 12:15pm

1969 LZ Grant... All our spare time we build a mess for chow and now a shower... The plans for the bunker feels important as the B52s keep getting closer with bombs that raise the dust in spastic motions as the Earth groans and we bounce...H

Feb 09, 2017 7:23pm

LZ Grant 1969... After two weeks the artillery going day and night I am in a tired haze wherein I can sleep through a barrage off the big cannons the 155s that lifts my sleeping pink and white body with the concussion as in my mind I run the sandy trails of North City West...H

Feb 09, 2014 8:43pm

69... With starlight scopes you could see the enemy building wired machine gun bunkers surrounding the LZ... They went underground at ease...They dressed in black and those who were captured swore they were massing for attack...H

Feb 09, 2012 8:48pm

VietNam 69... At this point I've had 2 premonitions of being wounded... Back in Del Mar, and again in Oklahoma, an intense dream wakes me and I've been shot in the mouth, the fabled "Million Dollar Wound" is said to be, "home with your balls"...H

Feb 10, 2013 8:04am

Viet Nam 69... People say why talk about it after all these years and I think that the same things were said to all vets from all wars and we stay quiet because unless you were there the truths hard to accept and wanting to be lovable keeps us from sharing what is unacceptable... But if the vets spoke would we rush down the same roads? Who really shows courage? The pacifist or the soldier? By now on LZGrant the loss of innocence was obvious and who/what we were evolving toward was not...H

Feb 10, 2018 9:46am

1969 LZ Grant... All our spare time we build a mess for chow and now a shower... The plans for the bunker feels important as the B52s keep getting closer with bombs that raise the dust in spastic motions as the Earth groans and we bounce...H

February, 1969   *They Owned the Night*

Feb 10, 2012 10:54am

VietNam 69... In the great Documentary, "War Dogs" a soldier says, "If they told you where you were going before you got there, you wouldn't go"... at LZ Grant captured enemy said we were surrounded and soon to die in a human wave assault...H

Feb 10, 2014 8:05pm

69... In chow line the guy behind me is from Escondido, surfs 15th street and for a minute we were back there, seagulls and all, wading together, I never saw the guy again... Daydream believer... I would get back to Del Mar...H

Feb 10, 2013 8:29pm

Viet Nam 69... An officer stopped by the gun to ask us if we'd heard the sounds of rooster crows? As a chicken rancher I said yes because I'd been noticing the sound for days, "How long has he been here?" he asked the crowd, he dismissed me, and told the others that the sound was from the enemy communications and to listen for it...H

Feb 11, 2012 8:30am

VietNam 69... Day by day my innocence ebbs, now that we know we're targeted to be wiped-out, it steeled our resolve and we fill sand bags by the hundreds, I vow to myself to get back to Del Mar and try to get back to being younger and playful...H

Feb 11, 2013 8:35am

Viet Nam 69... It seems every helicopter is coming here, we have extra ammo and now night-scopes, we need a sixth soldier on our gun, lots of infantry KIA's, but History has shown that the human wave assaults ended in 1967, right Charlie?...H

Feb 11, 2014 3:34pm

69... Staring at the radio in the middle of the night, "Somebody shoot her" says a voice, "F++K you, YOU shoot her"... by morning rumors were that a beauty strolled up to the guys, turned and strolled away... Mortars measured...H

Feb 11, 2016 7:29pm

1969... Weary to the bone, we wait for battle... As our enemy massed all around LZ Grant we shot down the biggest trees, we practiced with our M16's... We sang with Chicago, "We gotta get outta this place"...H

Feb 11, 2014 8:01pm

69... Stars were amazing from LZ Grant, the full moon was refreshingly familiar and Mankind was still 5 months away... All we wanted was to give Peace a chance, join the future, stop Warring... I suppose it was too much to ask...H

Feb 12, 2012 8:13am

VietNam 69... We should have 5 guys but we 4 are working...Presson and Bernard run the gun and me and Jones , labor... Presson is so selfish, the Army orders him to write his wife... Jones is a dolt... like all Bernards, Bernard is cool, mustache and all...H

February, 1969   *They Owned the Night*

Feb 12, 2013 8:23am

Viet Nam 69... It's so dark I can't see my hands but the guys using the starlight scopes see lots of enemy soldiers circling the LZ with commo wire and making machine gun bunkers all encircling us in the trap they are preparing, dedicated to Uncle Ho...H

Feb 12, 2014 8:53pm

69... If High School is one's boot camp, and Love being a battlefield.. I wrote from LZ Grant... "Libby, I Love you more Today than Yesterday but not as much as Tomorrow" and went back to the War...H

Feb 12, 2013 9:40pm

Viet Nam 69... With the meat grinder approaching LZ Grant, we grew pensive and outright grim, the Infantry said if we were overrun they'd take us with them and it seemed better than nothing, the burden of my generation had me in the danger zone, I remembered the handcuffed soldiers I'd seen in the airports... hummmmm...H

Feb 13, 2017 5:36am

LZ Grant... 69... Daydream... There were few fences between Black Mountain and the beach, with gentle rolling hills of sandy soils... and barefoot Summers had hot winds smelling of Eucalyptus, my first walk I headed for Forest Way... and sweet peas scented the air, the ladies in their bonnets waved me over for a sniff... and coos from the morning doves filled the soft sound of paradise... Boom...H

Feb 13, 2012 7:56am

VietNam 69... I'd bought Libby in the cheerleader auction, and I was getting my $ worth, but she and Bobby got going and I was gone... Her photo caused soldiers to go wild on LZ Grant... They married, Libby's sister was soon murdered by a Marine...H

Feb 13, 2013 8:56am

Viet Nam 69... Valentine's day brings our Sargent ordering the married guy on our gun to write home as his wife has received no letters and is complaining to the Army chain of command that he must be dead, no,... just busy dear...H

Feb 13, 2013 10:50pm

Viet Nam... 69... On the 25th anniversary of the battles of LZ Grant, 60 minutes' crew took along a few actual vets from 69 and in a few minutes they located and helped recover over 95 enemy soldiers' corpses in a mass grave on site...H

Feb 14, 2014 5:40am

69... The Russians say, "Never wake a sleeping bear"... we woke up to the fact that we were bait and became fighting son's of bitches, redoubling the bunker and preparing for the big one to come, the bear was in us the whole time...H

Feb 14, 2012 9:10am

VietNam 69... For me it was hard to believe we were surrounded, tunnels, what tunnels? We used our Artillery to blast away the bigger trees...

2 GIs were killed when the LZ's Jeep hit a newly planted mine inside our perimeter... Whats going on...H

Feb 14, 2014 6:33pm

69... PTSD? Nostalgia?... Why keep writing?...Lost souls searching for their graves or simply memories of virile youth?... I'm sure LZ Grant is ghostly every night after all the young lives lost there, my teeth join the Earth's hubris, so I write...H

Feb 15, 2013 5:52am

Viet Nam 69... It bothered us that LZ Grant was really nothing to die for... Even a small town or natural wonder would be better than this hell where the ants lust after the little chunks of life, and the fetid rot of the jungle, perfumes the humid air...H

Feb 15, 2018 5:55am

49 years ago I needed an M16... got shot, did some killing, left Viet Nam, and by gar I never again needed to own one and never will, that rifle is for War not Peace...H

Feb 15, 2012 8:16am

VietNam 69...At the North end of the LZ lies the remnants of a French Fort, just the foundation remains, our enemy has fought over this land for generations and have mapped coordinates for every inch, we're the center of the target, there it is...H

Feb 15, 2017 2:29pm

LZ Grant... 2017... Interviewing about Viet Nam ones awareness of public perceptions of War remain an image of some worth or proof of reasonable gains from killing enemy combatants... the ruthless historical model is as outmoded as the concept of "God's will be done"... veterans hope this antiquated form of abuse soon goes to the dust bin of history and progress brings PEACE...H

Feb 15, 2013 7:41pm

Viet Nam 69... The B52's are very close, with no moon the enemy will soon charge, we seem to be resigned to being the ducks on the pond, when the bombs get close its enough to rattle your dentures... I wanna go home...H

Feb 16, 2012 10:24am

VietNam 69... Enemy units are swarming to us like cats to a fish fry... Army brass issue us experimental ammo called "Co Fram", its artillery filled with bomblets that bounce off the ground and explode at 3 feet... I wanna go home Ma...H

Feb 16, 2015 11:25am

Fellow Viet Nam Vets Happy anniversary, 40 years over... We did our part in our generations burden... Under the same certainties, "America Love it or Leave it" I'd be going again, for the love of country...H

Feb 16, 2014 7:45pm

69... Teamwork made LZ Grant into the powerful defense still studied in America's War college... Among the biggest war stories of 1969... My ill fated tour had less than another week and I'd be done forever with LZ Grant...H

Feb 17, 2016 2:16am

1969... If I had a dog on LZ Grant... "Listen pal, I too know the Earth is shaking and I hate the booming Artillery, my food tastes like steel, and the Kool aid got old long ago... We'll make it buddy"...H

Feb 17, 2017 2:41am

LZ Grant 69... Still no mail from home, tempers are short and captured enemy soldiers say we will soon be attacked and killed as they overrun the position, infantry guys say they won't leave us but the thought of running thru the jungle brings no relief... Victory or death...H

Feb 17, 2013 9:21am

Viet Nam 69... We got our sixth crewman Today, Tom, a black guy whose first words were "I'm going to die here" and went down hill from there, eventually we put his babbling ass in the bunker as he was just in the way...H

Feb 17, 2012 9:58am

VietNam 69... Rumors are flying... We've been written off... The Infantry won't leave us behind... Chinese soldiers are leading the Vietnamese... we are the bait... they have tanks... they have antiaircraft weapons... they have flamethrowers.. shit...H

Feb 17, 2014 7:27pm

69... Many GI's never saw an enemy living soldier, I had, so can I go now? Only 335 days to go and I'm afraid of being captured so far in the jungle... Hey I'm afraid of this whole mess... Where's that summer of Love?...H

Feb 17, 2013 7:49pm

Viet Nam 69... Sitting on the shitter I see two American girls in pink stripes walking toward me, I freeze in embarrassment and lock eyes with one, she says 'Hello" so I give a weak wave and continue squeezing, public or not one must perform...H

Feb 18, 2012 8:03am

VietNam 69... A month ago we left the States on the plane me and Art Estrada, Jose Cisneros, Daniel Hackett (University of Florida grad)... Dan and Jose are KIA, Art gets the Bronze Star... At LZ Grant the calm has passed and here comes trouble...H

Feb 18, 2016 12:27pm

1969... B52's bomb so closely that everything starts shaking and the dust rises up from the Earth. The enemy's defenses are surrounding LZ Grant, we await our fate...H

Feb 18, 2014 6:42pm

69... Mortars from every compass point at sundown... Dust jerking upward from B-52s... Infantry says its coming... New artillery shells (Cofram) delivered, no-one knows how to use it (supposedly it bounces up and explodes)... the shits coming towards the fan...H

February, 1969 *They Owned the Night*

Feb 19, 2013 12:38am

Viet Nam 69... Mortars keep crashing down around LZ Grant, "They're bracketing us" say the vets, having fought before over these same acres, the NVA have the targets down flat, the first mortars all are landing in the perimeter, we return fire onto them...H

Feb 19, 2017 5:40am

LZ Grant... On February 23, 1969, I was wounded. A year later I was on a 30 day leave after an operation and me and Billy and Steve Gavin rode the train to Tepic and got off the train and rode a taxi to San Blas and 24 dollars later we were in the tropics and warm water changed everything as I surfed and everything was permanently altered for the better...H

Feb 19, 2013 8:29am

Viet Nam 69... Our radio call sign is "Birth Control" for the 77th, we shoot for the 2nd 12th, Inf Ist Cav, their 4 platoons are radio tagged as, A, B, C, D, or "Ace High, Bad Bet, Wild Card and Stacked Deck" we're gamblers alright with everything on the line...H

Feb 19, 2012 9:02am

VietNam 69... We get a replacement, Tom... He says "I'm gonna die here... I've come here to die... oh no no no I'ma gonna die right here... All this way from home and now I'm here to die" we put him in the bunker 'cause he was useless...H

Feb 19, 2014 6:25pm

69... The vets say we got bracketed for tonight by the mortars, I hate the bunker, its like a grave, and too much thumping in dust, if I die down there I'll never forgive myself... The world began when I was born, or was Shakespeare right that you can't wash blood away?...H

Feb 19, 2012 8:04pm

VietNam 69... The glorious Infantry rings the Artillery on LZ Grant... So far this Feb., soldiers were struck by Malaria, heat stroke, fevers, snake-bites, accidental discharges, bullets, shrapnel, a man went berserk, bamboo cuts, booby traps, pungi stakes, and some rotated stateside. Artillery is like kissing your girlfriend...H

Feb 20, 2016 2:04am

1969... Being expendable creates bitter soldiers, I mean there was nothing strategic about LZ Grant, a few years ago Grant Larson went to the spot and saw a fertile manioc farm. On February 21 Army reports the probing began with 6 sappers, beginning what would be one of the biggest battle stories of 1969... LZ Grant, rest in hell...H

Feb 20, 2017 4:59am

LZ Grant... We're told to get our M-16s to practice and shoot shoot shoot... because with no moon the massive Army of North Viet Nam will come up out of the ground tunnels, raging mad and seeking American blood as first they probe with sappers and use the massive 220 mm mortar they lugged through the jungle... They want to wipe us out...H

Feb 20, 2013 7:40am

Viet Nam 69... I often wonder just what the leaders said to inspire, the NVA had decided to not do more human wave assaults back in '66, the vets from LZ Grant have long claimed Chinese soldiers were mixed with the dead, but they don't talk... Close...H

February, 1969 *They Owned the Night*

Feb 20, 2012 7:59am

VietNam 69... Our enemy has ringed us with machine guns/fighting positions they are preparing the anti-aircraft weapons and topping off their flamethrowers... They pour out of their tunnels dedicated to "Uncle Ho"... we 220 were locked and loaded...H

Feb 20, 2014 1:46pm

69... Jets being struck by anti-aircraft guns circle us and unleash a tumbling bomb that rattles one's teeth... We are shooting a pattern to clear our front, the world began when I was born, my world right now is a world of hurt, I wanna go home!...H

Feb 20, 2013 3:34pm

Viet Nam 69... The evening of the 22nd the Infantry quickly recalled all the soldiers who manned the listening posts and observation posts because they reported being aware of enemy soldiers throughout our area coming up out of tunnels...H

Feb 21, 2018 12:05am

Viet Nam left me facially wounded and grouped together with men missing parts from the shoulder up, missing a nose or the whole face we were messed up and unlikely to succeed but the first night home I smoked a joint for the first time in my life, made love to my girl friend and was the happiest I've ever been... 49 years later I give credit to marijuana to helping me get healthy and serene, and of course Trump says no way for pot and Veterans to do research so the new Vets with 20 per cent suffering from PTSD and 22 a day commit suicide but Trump the traitor and indeed San Diego supervisors are unwilling to honor the vote of the citizens about recreational use... Peace...H

The Living Ghosts

Feb 21, 2016 12:47am

1969... Even after 2 premonitions of being shot in the mouth, I didn't know the date. February 23rd was somehow going to answer all my questions even before I spit out all that mush of teeth and bone...H

Feb 21, 2017 5:19am

LZ Grant... Among the biggest combat stories from 1969, tonight was my last on the LZ, what followed is a long studied defense from repeated ground attacks or human waves of devoted soldiers who died for their cause... I salute their bravery and thank the Americans who served that era with all we had, dog faces or devil dogs, Americans...H

Feb 21, 2012 8:06am

VietNam 69... Listenup... No moon tonight... ther'e gonna hit us.. Keep your fucking helmet strapped on... Don't let the powder build up... If we need beehive rounds or white phosphorous, you be ready, we got no armor the uniform will save you...H

Feb 21, 2013 9:43am

Viet Nam 69... At this point, on the cusp of War its almost like sex, all engrossing, heightened awareness, dedicated to the moment, never been so alive, never wanted to live more, never loved Life quite this way, want eternity to want me alive...H

Feb 21, 2012 12:46pm

VietNam...69... Listenup... After you write your name inside your boots... we'll do a "mad minute" 5 minutes after sundown, shoot everything we got and hit everything high, with Tom safe in the bunker, we were ready to rock and roll...H

Feb 21, 2016 1:41pm

1969... Waking up in a hospital covered in ants, I had no idea how hurt I was, until I looked in the mirror, looking back at me was someone I didn't recognize. The 2 NVA next to me seemed oblivious to my presence and the GI across from me was determined to die...H

Feb 21, 2012 3:56pm

VietNam 69... As you know we moved up the "Mad Minute" so to get the teams out to listen and observe, we're calling them back in because its a target rich environment, "Spooky" the gunship is flying here, we start firing a few minutes (boom).

Feb 21, 2012 6:47pm

VietNam 69... 43 years ago Today, the army saying goes "Hurry up and wait 'cause the Army is 99% boredom and 1% action"...well here comes the 1%, by this Time Tomorrow my Life was altered, forever... And away we go...H

Feb 21, 2014 8:19pm

69... Last day on LZ Grant, tonight we dance with the devil, we're all in, too late to change fates, its time to grin and bear it... Love America, even if you can't agree with combat in Viet Nam, its Time to perform, so shut the fuck up...H

Feb 22, 2013 1:25am

   Viet Nam 69... Everybody listen up! I want your 16's next to the bunker, leave Tom in there, fully loaded magazines, put your helmet chin straps on, tonights the night we're going to rock and roll and there's no where to go from LZ Grant...H

Feb 22, 2012 5:24am

   VietNam 69... At last night's twilight Presson was back to drawing, Jones was trimming his 'stach, Bernard was chatting up anyone when BAM mortar on the North BAM on the West BAM on the East... "Bracketing us" said Top... Jesse Montez of San Antonio Texas was the first to die...H

Feb 22, 2017 6:05am

   Hey Joe where you going with that gun in your hand? Into an ambush in a foreign land, Joe bled out in Viet Nam, my friend died from a booby trap, joining 58 thousand bloodied corpses, and missing out on life, his sister heartbroken, his town torn, his nation lost spun into chaos by a bullshit war... Jose B Cisneros rest in peace my brother... July 12, 1969...H

Feb 22, 2014 6:09am

   69... Tom just got here, went unstable and now he's in the bunker, useless, low on ammo out of water, we can hear more than we can see, but what do we do once the ammo's gone.... shoulda joined the Navy...H

Feb 22, 2012 8:14am

   VietNam 69... We've been firing a pattern for hours we're super thirsty and half the ammo's gone, I check the radio, "Radio-check?" and "Who are you?" comes back, "I'm gun 5 of the 105's" I say, and I was never more serious in my life...H

Feb 22, 2013 9:19am

Viet Nam 69...Enemy mortars are falling wily-nilly or helter skelter since sundown, one hit the 155's and the Texan from San Antonio, Jesse Montez was shredded and killed, now its personal, remember Tonight, if it walks like a duck, kill it...H

Feb 22, 2012 9:55am

VietNam 69... Teamwork gets the 3 grunts back inside our lines, an officer asks me to run ammo to the right of our position to gun 6... I make it the first time but not the second, "So thats what it feels like to be shot" first thought in a vast darkness...H

Feb 22, 2012 11:11am

VietNam... 69 vast darkness, but my instincts tell me its familiar.. "Have you lived long enough?" Uh no..."Do you want to go back?" Uh yes.. and 'poof' I was back at LZ Grant, Presson was hovering over me saying "Hold still I'll clear your mouth"...H

Feb 22, 2013 3:12pm

Viet Nam 69... With "Spooky" flying a tight circle above the LZ we've passed many hours shooting a pattern of direct fire, barrels down, on the radio I hear 3 US soldiers outside the wire... and they luckily are in front of me as we make contact on the radio...H

The Living Ghosts

Feb 22, 2018 4:21pm

Yes 49 years ago tonight when the North Vietnamese Army attacked and after hours of combat I was running ammo when shrapnel tore me a new one, I was unconscious and a voice asked... "Have you lived long enough?...Do you want to go back?"... it was peaceful and natural... I seemed detached resting there awaiting a helicopter, and shadows fall, and darkness disappears in flashes of explosions... and then cool air as the helicopter took off and the red hot Landing Zone Grant faded to black... February 23, 1969... Forever yours...H

Feb 22, 2014 6:08pm

69... In desperation I strike a Faustian bargain, my teeth for a helicopter ride out... Hours later I feel sheets and my leaden body tries to awaken only to see ants swarming on my eyes... Hospital yeah but off LZ GRANT!...H

Feb 22, 2012 6:34pm

Viet Nam... 69... To the guys putting me on the medi-vac I looked like a guy who'd bought the farm and was cashing in his chips or to go kick the can... We flew outa there like a bat from hell... At the hospital they cut off my boot to read my name...H

Feb 22, 2013 7:01pm

Viet Nam 69... 3 guys are in, we did it... I'm ordered to take ammo to the weak spot to our North, I do it and then... I feel myself inside a blackness, and I hear a voice ask me crystal clear, "Have you lived long enough?" Oh shit "Do you want to go back?"...H

February, 1969 *They Owned the Night*

Feb 22, 2013 8:37pm

Viet Nam 69... Feeling sheets I tried to open my eyes, but couldn't, but the ants on my eyelids powered a second try, and I found myself standing up, "Hey" I hear, but by now I see a mirror, and look at some poor schmuck who is a mess, he moves as I move so I figure thats really me... Heading home... Thanks everybody...H

Feb 22, 2014 8:47pm

69... One more... At impact I went outa here, in a familiar dimension/world, I hear a voice... "have you lived long enough?" and then, "Would you like to go back?"... As an agnostic at heart, I've pondered that one...H

Feb 22, 2012 9:46pm

VietNam 69... Sheets, my feet feel sheets, I try for a long Time to open my eyes only to see ants swarming on me... Oh well its not LZ Grant and it's a start... Hey Thank You to all my friends for taking this trip down memory lane with me...H

Feb 23, 2012 5:23am

Epilogue... LZ Grant on the 25th anniversary of the battles of LZ Grant, CBS' 60 Minutes sent Steven Croft to the site, thus rekindling my interests, they helped in the recovery of 100 (give or take) enemy soldiers in the mass grave near the French Fort...H

Feb 23, 2016 8:49am

1969... Dulled with a concussion I arrived in San Diego weighing 138lbs... The 2 weeks in Japan would forever be fuzzy and seeing eucalyptuses as we landed at Miramar is my first clear memory of being welcomed home...H

Feb 23, 2013 8:53am

Viet Nam 69... Home at last weight 138lbs...We drove down the sandy driveway, and I most wanted to see the dogs, so I got out to greet my friends properly, same with my girlfriend, who went with me to the apricot orchard to practice wrestling...H

Feb 24, 2014 6:35pm

I came really close, A long Time ago... of being just another name, another G. I. Joe... Killed in youth, and forever dead, devoid of Glory just dead instead... I say their names, Jose B Cisneros, Daniel H Hackett, and 58,000 others...H

Feb 25, 2012 7:41am

42 years ago Today... Bitter and disillusioned, "alienated"... this bird flew the cage only to chain myself to the sky... with the Earth my living room, and the Universe my view... the Army was over and I'd done my part in the collective burden of Vietnam...H

LZ Grant Arc Light, By Mark Schlageter

MARCH, 1969

A PICASSO IN PROGRESS.

Mar 02, 2016 9:35am

1969... Arrived in San Diego, Balboa Naval Hospital, girl friend greeting leads to fun time in the vast gardens, ah yes good ol' Libby, makes a man feel appreciated...H

Mar 12, 2018 3:42am

Twas 49 years ago today, the hospital plane flew toward Miramar and I saw Eucalyptus trees as we lowered and as soon as possible I put a dime in a pay phone and called home, with my tracheotomy I couldn't speak but my brother answered and of course he knew it was me... Bused to Balboa Naval Hospital where I embraced my girlfriend, found a quiet place and humped away... in America, long live the United States...H

The Living Ghosts

Mar 12, 2016 12:56am

So today our nation honors Vietnam vets, and we thank our fellow Americans. It still floors me to see constant scams done in our name, from the Wounded Warriors to literally dozens more, we need the government to assist the disabled. Its been an interesting road, being drafted into an Army full of Americans that were a mix of college grads and high school dropouts. We put aside our differences, assumed a common burden, worked together, and faced the music... I learned a lot and was a better man afterwards...H

Mar 15, 2013 8:25am

I had to smile when the doctor Today said, "This'll leave a scar on your face"...I told him my face is, "A Picasso in progress." and so he got it done...H

Mar 19, 2018 2:58am

Twas 49 years ago today, my friends slipped me out of the hospital and took me to the Del Mar ranch... In Viet Nam I decided to stay put on the 212 acres of rolling, sandy hills and cooing doves with cottontails abounding and a cool soft breeze, and then my girlfriend got me stoned, we made love and I was the happiest I've ever been, home again and firmly embraced by the green green grass of home...H

Mar 26, 2018 9:33am

March 1969... Weeks after Viet Nam I was introduced to this man, he was putting on his dress blues and proud of himself, he turned to meet me and stared off to the side, muttered a few consonants and left the ward on a thirty day leave, about twenty years later I saw him and asked how he was doing... "I had a vasectomy and I've got a Master Card so I'm ready to go"... what doesn't kill you can make you stronger...H

March, 1969   A Picasso in Progress

Mar 29, 2016 10:03am

Viet Nam vets, how do you handle the phony vets? Generally their stories expose themselves quickly, I ask,"What was your unit" and go from there. They leave me as fast as they can get away zooooooooom...H

DEPARTMENT OF THE ARMY
HEADQUARTERS 1ST CAVALRY DIVISION (AIRMOBILE)
APO San Francisco 96490

3 June 1969

GENERAL ORDERS
NUMBER 7000

AWARD OF THE ARMY COMMENDATION MEDAL FOR HEROISM

1. TC 320. The following AWARD is announced.

FISHER, HOWARD L. US56732344 (556-78-8663) PRIVATE FIRST CLASS United States Army Battery C, 1st Battalion (Airmobile), 77th Artillery

Awarded: Army Commendation Medal with "V" Device
Date Action: 23 February 1969
Theater: Republic of Vietnam
Reason: For heroism in connection with military operations against a hostile force in the Republic of Vietnam. Private First Class Fisher distinguished himself by heroism in action on 23 February 1969, while serving as a cannoneer with Battery C, 1st Battalion (Airmobile), 77th Artillery during an enemy attack. When his unit's perimeter came under an intense enemy rocket, mortar and ground attack, Private First Class Fisher exposed himself to the hostile fire as he acted as radio-telephone operator for his section, relaying data for counter mortar and direct fire on the enemy positions. With complete disregard for his own safety Private First Class Fisher then carried ammunition to his section. In so doing, he was seriously wounded. His display of personal bravery and devotion to duty is in keeping with the highest traditions of the military service, and reflects great credit upon himself, his unit and the United States Army.
Authority: By direction of the Secretary of the Army, under the provisions Army Regulation 672-5-1.

OFFICIAL:

ROY M. TRAUGOTT
1LT, AGC
Asst AG

ROBERT M. SHOEMAKER
Colonel, GS
Chief of Staff

DISTRIBUTION:
2 - AG-ASD
10 - AVYAL-G-AD
2 - AVDIAG-R
1 - G1

This document was retyped due to damage and difficulty to read.

APRIL, 1969

THAT ROTTEN WAR.

Apr 06, 2018 2:42am

April 6 1970... Last day in Army... Retiring after medical discharge, grandmother says... "Twenty years old and a pension? Well, you'll never amount to anything"... smart lady... Now in 2018, 3rd week begins for Grant Larson in induced coma, time is precious... it goes too fast... Go Grant go...H

Apr 07, 2012 8:31am

I'll never forget the draft notice said August 28... 6AM... the Ranch was so quiet I could hear dad grinding his teeth, as the dew drops formed in the Eucalyptus, and dropped in groups, reassuring me that it was time to go, the Ranch was timeless...H

Apr 24, 2013 1:53pm

Mottled moon light through the Oak forest, makes my whistles echo with spookiness as I tried to see what the ruckus was about, the shriek of a coyote brought chills as they all started in to scream at me, outnumbered again a la Viet Nam, but they aren't shooting, whew... Julian is hard on women and dogs...H

April, 1969   That Rotten War

Apr 30, 2015 8:57am

    Jose B Cisneros, died July 12th 1969, we would've been friends for life if only he'd survived that rotten War. Same for my friend, Daniel Hackett (who sang Bob Dylan songs throughout boot camp) he believed he was under the radar of our man's Army... A rebel at heart, but still dead... ...H

MAY, 1969

WHERE I CAN BE FREE.

May 23, 2013 9:33pm

Yo America, memorial day for me brings back to Life Jose B. Cisneros a gentle soldier I was amigos with who bled to death from multiple wounds... and Daniel Hackett, a University of Florida grad who didn't get a job, got drafted and again bled out in Viet Nam... 1,000 guys a month were dying... Never forget them...H

May 24, 2015 12:06pm

In '67 100,000 Americans marched on the pentagon grounds to protest the escalation of the Viet Nam war... A year later I was in country and grateful for the memory... Today's headline... "Back to Iraq"... silence from the people... Back to a war where we are flat out beaten... The people have no voice here..........H

May 25, 2014 8:21pm

68... Del Mar was blithesome... yet August 27th, at 6 AM in Oceanside, I was to meet the bus to start my way across this world, and then if I'm Lucky, back to Del Mar from which I never had wanted to leave in the first place... oy vey...H

May 26, 2013 8:15am

My friend, John Baca (medal of honor) gets a standing ovation from all the different crowds he appears in front of. Yesterday at our Wounded Warriors breakfast I got a standing ovation... and I like saying it felt pretty good, thanks Roy Wathen...H

May 27, 2018 7:39pm

I nearly died in combat, my friend Jose B Cisneros did... We were both out of place in the macho Army, drawn together by loving to laugh at jokes from Arthur Estrada... Gentle and kind Joe had our back and a booby trap killed him July 12, 1969... Hey Joe where you gonna go with that gun in your hand... Way down to Mexico where I can be free.

May 29, 2017 3:22am

The family running to the freed POW is fatherhood personified positively... Twas 1973 and I was back in the Naval Hospital on the plastic surgery second floor and we watched the limos in line deliver the men after North Viet Nam held them all those years... A raucous crowd and happy Americans... For us it was the end of the war... Happy Father's Day America...H

May 30, 2016 10:11am

    I met an old soldier 70 years old who spoke of his war in the present tense even though his was in 1966, service of 18 months, and his scared head shook with pleasure when I told him he was my brother, it was like looking in the mirror...H

The End

ABOVE
Left to Right: Bernard, Presson, Jones.

BELOW
Apocalypse Now

Army Driver's License

Morning shot on LZ Grant

Our gun, a 102mm Howitzer.

Gun 5 with a simple trench for bunker.

Early morning chow line.

The conjoined tails of our 102 version of a standard 105mm.

Perimiter with the jungle in the background.

The U.S. flag, solidly sandbagged into place, flutters over an American artillery position near Bien Hoa as troopers unpack shells during heavy fighting in the area. (UPI Radiophoto)

Me and Jones.

Jones and mustache.

PACIFIC STARS AND STRIPES

and Duel Rages

Monday, March 10, 1969 — 10¢

Vol. 25, No. 68 — AN AUTHORIZED PUBLICATION OF THE U.S. Armed Forces in the Far East

GIs Hurl Back Charge By N. Viet Battalion

By JO2 DAVE WARSH
S&S Vietnam Bureau

SAIGON — A battalion of well-equipped North Vietnamese soldiers — some of them carrying flame-throwers — charged an isolated U.S. landing zone early Saturday but crumbled as the little camp's howitzers were fired at them like rifles.

The attack on the 1st Air Cav. Div.'s Landing Zone Grant, about 45 miles northwest of Saigon, was coupled with two other unsuccessful assaults on American bases along Communist corridors to the capital.

Meanwhile, Communist gunners opened up overnight on some 50 targets scattered throughout Vietnam. Most of the shellings were aimed at small military units, U.S. spokesmen said. Few casualties and only light damage was reported.

Some larger units also were hit, the spokesmen said, and the Communists apparently reserved the heaviest of their shellings for the U.S. Marine combat base at An Hoa, about 20 miles southwest of Da Nang. About 135 mortar and rocket rounds hit the camp, causing light casual-

(Continued on Back Page, Col. 3)

An Israeli soldier inspects a missile taken from the wreckage of an Egyptian MIG downed during a dogfight over the Sinai Desert Saturday. also was shot d...

Astronauts Turn 'Space Focus on Earth's Riches

SPACE CENTER, Houston (AP) — Their dangerous Apollo 9 orbiting over, the three astronauts took on a new job Saturday. They prospected the earth for 100 miles in space hidden riches from With special cameras aimed precisely at special ground targets, the astronauts hope to pick up clues to mineral resources, water, timberlands, and fishing grounds by the special light radiations they emit.
But they ran into small difficulties on their first attempt because of an error by mission control.
As Air Force Cols. James A. McDivitt and David R. Scott and civilian Russell L. Schweick-art trained their filtered cameras on the American Southwest, they noticed the automatic pilot was turning the ship the wrong way.
Mission control quickly gave permission for manual flight, and after checking, sheepishly reported it had given the wrong autopilot information.
But before they turned to their task, they took time off to sing "Happy Birthday" to the flight operations director, Christopher Columbus Kraft Jr., the man in mission control who shepherded every U.S. manned flight.
As the astronauts sped into the last and easiest half of their 10-day mis...

Stars and Stripes article on LZ Grant. Discussed in the next article from Vietnam Magazine. Pg. 96.

Reds Hurled Back

(Continued From Page 1)

ties and damage. Artillery pieces fired back, but it is unknown if any Reds were hit.

Other shellings included 15 mortar and rocket rounds fired at the base camp of a brigade of the 25th Inf. Div. at Dau Tieng, about 40 miles northwest of Saigon, and early morning and afternoon shellings Saturday at the base camp of the U.S. 9th Inf. Div. in Dong Tam, 35 miles southwest of the capital. No casualties were reported at either site.

Allied military experts had predicted the "second phase" of the Reds' spring offensive over the weekend. Still, there was no confirmation that this was it.

If and when it does come, military authorities generally agree that it will be in the form of more of the same: mortar and rocket attacks on military installations and cities, and ground attacks on Allied bases.

At least 77 Communists' bodies were left on the battlefield at Landing Zone Grant, a brush-covered plain in the shadow of Mt. Ba Den, about 15 miles northeast of Tay Ninh City. There were indications that well over 100 Reds had died in the midnight fight but that the survivors had carried many bodies away.

The fighting began at the landing zone moments after a heavy mortar barrage. One huge 120-mm mortar shell crashed through the roof of the operations center, killing the camp commander and three others.

Seven other GIs died and 30 were wounded defending the landing zone.

Although some Communists carried flame-throwers, apparently none got close enough to use them. Two of the napalm-loaded weapons were captured, along with a small antiaircraft gun and scores of other weapons used in the attack.

Maj. Billy Brown, 30, who took command of the camp after the commander was killed, said the rifle company that defended the camp fought so well that most of the Claymore mines ringing the camp were not needed and were not fired.

Air strikes and Spooky gunships peppered the Reds as they charged and the camp's defenders lowered their artillery pieces and fired point-blank into the on-rushing Reds.

At least six Communists made it through two rings of concertina barbwire to die less than 30 feet from the guns of the cavalry troopers. None made it through the final defenses.

In June, 2006 'Vietnam Magazine' published the following article by Howard Fisher detailing the brave defense of LZ Grant.

DEFENDING LZ GRANT

An Army captain interrupted my slumber by tapping on my shoulder. "Let's go!" he commanded, and pushed my wheelchair through the hospital doors, toward a huge jet. He stayed within arm's reach for the next seven hours. The captain was very sullen. Unable to speak, I wrote him a note: "Why are you here?"

"Because," he said slowly, "you're almost dead."

It was my 43rd day in Vietnam, early in March 1969, and Saigon's usually oppressive heat for once felt warn and welcome. In the bright sun of the morning I left my wheelchair and shuffled behind the captain, up the wide stairs at the back of the massive hospital plane.

We must have been among the last to board, and the plane looked packed. Recently wounded soldiers lay in all the berths on both sides of the aisles. With the captain holding the intravenous bottles whose lines were hooked into my arm, it was slow going through the crowd, and our seats were at the front of the plane. Most of the injured were burn patients, who were bandaged from head to toe. They made not a sound. I was ambulatory but was unable to see my own injuries. I felt like a voyeur among those shattered soldiers. Once we were seated, the lack of windows made it hard to tell exactly when the lurching jet's wheels lifted off the ground of South Vietnam.

Seven hours later we landed in Japan, and I felt lucky to be singled out for helicopter transport to Camp Drake, home of the 249th General Hospital. The flight took us over what looked like a Third World country, with shacks crowding every bit of land. Once the aircraft landed, the captain signed off his cargo-me-and waved goodbye. Among Japan's snowy grounds and bleak gray skies, Vietnam seemed forgotten and very far away.

The hospital wards were the size of warehouses. There were crowds of patients, and with only a few overworked nurses, the wounded were nearly on their own. I discovered an out-of-the-way, spa-sized bathtub where, after 10 days, I was finally able to clean my bloody scalp and body. Other than immense hunger, I really felt all right.

Head wounds were the common theme in my section of the ward. Across from me, a recently blinded warrant officer, who was missing the right front of his skull, frequently got up to walk beside his bed. Soon he was entangled in medical equipment, and he would smile and laugh at his problems. To my side was a very talkative and very much wounded Marine, whose every appendage hung in a sling. His story was of being shot in the legs, then falling exposed on the battlefield. Every time he moved he was peppered with bullets and fragments. Nurses were always bent over his bed attending to his wounds. One day I watched my left hand reach out and feel a nurse's bottom; it surprised me, and I caught hell from her! The next day, my name appeared on the manifest of those who were to be sent Stateside on March 11, 1969.

While looking for reading material for the flight, I grabbed the Pacific edition of Stars and Stripes. The paper was dated Monday, March 10, 1969, and its headline read "GIs Hurl Back Charge by N. Viet Battalion," by JO2 Dave Warsh. The article began:

Saigon- A battalion of well-equipped North Vietnamese soldiers- some of them carrying flame-throwers-charged an isolated U.S. landing zone early Saturday, but crumbled as the little camp's howitzers were fired at them like rifles.

The attack on the 1st Air Cav Div's Landing Zone Grant, about 45 miles northwest of Saigon, was coupled with two other unsuccessful assaults on American bases along Communist corridors to the capital....

Landing Zone Grant was the same place I'd been wounded, and after some weeks in the confines of antiseptic hospitals, it shocked me to realize my old unit was still in the midst of that hell on earth.

Hard-learned lessons from the 1968 Tet Offensive had led the U.S. military to order blocking force on Vietnamese highways before Tet 1969. LZ Grant was built across Highway 13, which connected Saigon to Cambodia. With two batteries of American artillery and the 2nd Battalion, 12th Infantry (2-12 Inf), all in place, the road was closed.

LZ Grant was built next to the foundation of a long-gone French fort. Outer and inner concertina wire protected the infantry, which was supported by artillery. Six 155mm howitzers manned by A/1-30 artillery formed a semicircle on the east side of Highway 13, and our own six 105mm howitzers completed the circle on the west side. LZ Grant was still being constructed, and an ancient antitank mine killed an American operating a bulldozer only an hour before I was airlifted in as a replacement.

C Battery, 1st Battalion, 77th Artillery (C/1-77), had assigned me to a five-man howitzer crew near the end of January 1969. William Perry was the section chief, the gunner was George Presson, and the other cannoneers were named Jones and Bernard. They all had spent months with the 77th and always kidded me for plugging my ears when the howitzers fired. After some weeks with them, I felt the LZ was home and the crew was family. They told me that no soldier in the 77th had been killed since last April, and that sounded reassuring.

Presson kept us toiling, building a bunker next to our gun and filling endless sandbags. Harassment and interdiction fire (H&I) on the intersections of potential enemy trails required day and night firing. The area was very active with the NVA. We fired so much that when we slept, the concussions from our howitzers did not awaken us. A good day for our crew was rewarded at twilight with one soda and one beer. During our fire missions, the sounds and the cordite smells were exhilarating. Each time we pulled the lanyard, we almost never knew just who it was we were saving or killing.

Outside the landing zone's perimeter, the jungle grew 30 feet tall with a mixture of grass, brush and trees. Every day, infantry patrols discovered huge caches of rice or military supplies. When B-52s bombed the surrounding jungle, dust would rise across the LZ in a choking ripple. At noon every day, both sides observed an unofficial cease-fire for an hour. We looked forward to the break. One day at 1308 hours, three NVA soldiers, looking at a clipboard, were spotted just outside the wire. Somebody counted down from 10 on the radio system, and at zero, mortars and everything else the infantry had were fired at the three. The blasts lifted them maybe five feet into the air, and their bodies arched up and turned from the impact. They dropped from view into the waist-high grass as an American infantry squad raced out to the positions, but the GIs found no bodies. We concluded that subterranean tunnels like honeycombs beneath the ground were enabling the NVA to encroach on our positions. The infantry later found tunnel entrances near the old French fort.

On February 23, 1969, our twilight routine was interrupted by mortar rounds incoming from both sides of the jungle. We scurried into our bunkers, then after a few rounds only quiet followed. The word from the infantry was of enemy activity around the entire LZ. The 200 Americans on LZ Grant locked and loaded every weapon they had. It was quiet until midnight, when a renewed mortar barrage began, and the NVA advanced in a mass assault.

Flares popped into the sky, hanging from parachutes and illuminating the battlefield, revealing a target-rich environment. Both forces opened fire. The NVA's .51-caliber machine gun dominated the first minute of the action as it swept the LZ with its green tracers. Our dug-in infantrymen were raking out fields of fire from relative darkness, while the NVA troops were scrambling to stay alive above ground in near-daylight brightness.

We held our ground and waited for an AC-130 Spooky gunship to circle the LZ. The plane kept the NVA moving, and the .51-caliber went quiet. The Spooky had enormous amounts of ammunition, and its Gatling guns rained down a twisting line of orange tracers. We watched in awe. Fighter jets swooped down to deliver huge bombs, and Cobra helicopter gunships fired rockets, machine gun rounds and grenades down at the exposed NVA. The smaller light observation helicopter's guns were deadly as well. The NVA seemed to have little chance to survive. Eventually the Spooky ran out of ammunition and winged away to re-arm. Five minutes later NVA lanterns were moving in the jungle as the enemy prepared to attack.

We shared the landing zone with the 2-12 Infantry, which used the radio call signs Ace High, Bad Bet and Daddy Rabbit. The 2-12 was deployed around the LZ and fought bravely. Artillery backed the infantry. We immediately lowered the tubes nearly level, firing directly at pointblank range. We shot all our beehive rounds, then all our white phosphorus - and still the NVA charged. At that point: we began to fire high-explosive rounds, using one increment of powder and setting the fuzes to super-quick. In the process, we quickly piled up an enormous number of excess powder bags near the guns, which we were afraid would go off. By that time too we were all nearly deaf. I was exhausted.

When things started to calm down a bit, I crawled into my hooch and instantly fell asleep. AK-47 fire from about 100 yards away soon woke me. By then we were low on all types of ammo, and the beehive rounds were long gone.

The battery telephone system connected all the guns with the fire direction center (FDC); the chief of firing battery, a Sergeant Rabb; and the battery commander, a Captain Capshaw. The commo system had been useless throughout most of the battle, with only static on the Line. Nonetheless I thought l should try a commo check, and I was amazed to make contact with three GIs. Caught outside the wire, the men were a listening post for the infantry. They were overjoyed to establish contact and asked me my position. Recognizing our gun's number, they were sure they were right to our front. They asked us to fire a round so they would know where we were. We alerted the infantry and somehow they got their men back inside the wire.

By this time the NVA were overrunning the old French fort's foundation, and we lost time searching for the wire to detonate the pre-positioned explosive charges. As the NVA advanced to our outer concertina wire, an officer I'd never seen before jumped into our gun position and took cover on the ground, lying alongside the wall of sandbags. He searched our faces, looked me in the eyes and asked, "Which of you is the freshest?"

I had been on the radio long enough to stop sweating and I answered, "I am."

The officer ordered me to carry ammunition to a howitzer 20 yards up the road, aimed at the fort's ruins. The gun was exposed, a little below the road's shoulder. Loaded down with amino, I ran up the highway to the cannon. The crew was visible, lying in the lee of their howitzer. As I approached I could hear fragments and bullets passing menacingly close. So much steel was in the air that I clumped the shells next to the prone soldiers and then asked the closest man, "How much ammo do you have?"

A furious soldier yelled, "We got what you brought."

I'd delivered three 50-pound rounds, so there was my answer. I turned and ran. Huffing down the road, I saw an officer belly-crawling toward me in the roadside ditch. As I spoke to him he stared expressionless, and I hurried around the turn that led to my gun. Breathlessly, I relayed my information to the officer who had sent me on the mission, and with no hesitation he asked, "Would you go again?"

It was a question, not an order, but as I paused to consider it, Presson started loading me up again with rounds at nearly 50 pounds each, one in each hand and one across my back. That load was too heavy to allow me to crouch, and at 6 feet 4 inches I had been lucky to make it the first time. After reaching the howitzer, I paused to collect my breath and suddenly felt something like a kick to my mouth. I flew backwards, head first. So that's what it feels like to get shot, I thought.

Everything went black, yet I was aware of my existence, and in a familiar void. A voice asked, "Have you lived long enough?"

No, I thought, I had not, and I willed my silent "No!"

"Do you want to go back?" the voice asked.

Yes, I do, I thought and suddenly regained consciousness after maybe two seconds had passed. I was now on my knees and

Presson was telling me to hold still so he could clear my mouth. I had no idea what he was talking about. I reached up to my mouth and touched steel. Somehow I said, "I can do it," then pulled out the metal, scooped away my teeth with my fingers and tried to breathe.

The fragment was shaped like a hockey puck. It had caved in my mouth and come to a stop by crushing through my teeth. My lower jawbone halted it before my throat. I was quite aware, and I recognized the piece of metal as a base-plate of an artillery round. The American friendly fire was probably part of a supporting barrage from other firebases within our range. At times like these the shelling was brought in as close as possible, even on the outer perimeter, and fragmentation often blew back onto our positions.

The battery medic appeared with a stretcher. He ducked his head as dust and dirt blew everywhere. I tossed aside the fragment I had dug out of my mouth and crawled onto the stretcher. I was surprised to see a medevac helicopter hovering on the road about 75 feet away. GIs quickly strapped me into place on the chopper's flank, above somebody with leg wounds. My head was toward the tail of the helicopter, and I was lying on my belly so I was dripping a lot of blood on the man below me. His hands were covering his face, and he looked to see what was dripping on him, then grimaced and lurched to the side. As the pilots increased the rotor's rpms, the soldier looked at me again with a horrified expression. I made an obscene gesture, something I've regretted ever since.

As we took to the air I felt a cool wind, and I watched as the entire American force opened fire in our support. The hellhole LZ was alive and glowed a deadly orange as it grew smaller, before disappearing into the darkness of the jungle. We landed at a Cu Chi field hospital where the staff rushed the wounded into the MASH unit. My dog tags were missing, and I could not speak. A blonde nurse cut off my boots so they could identify me from the information written inside. She attached a tag to my fatigue shirt and told me that I was too severely injured to be treated there. She said I would be reloaded onto a medevac and flown to the 24th Evacuation Hospital near Saigon. As soldiers carried me out, I flashed the peace sign to the nurses. Their sad faces made me think I must have looked pretty bad.

The Living Ghosts

I waited through the night as the doctors treated a mass of casualties. Dozens of soldiers with head wounds circulated through a warehouse-like reception area for surgery. Medics prepared the wounded for the surgeons. For most soldiers, that required the shaving of their heads. A few of the men were talkative, even giddy. Morphine cannot be used for head wounds; the men probably felt a natural high from adrenaline and the excitement of surviving combat. As the hours wore on, a medic told me to be patient. He said that my injuries would take too much of the doctor's time, and asked me to hide my face with a towel for the sake of the other soldiers' morale. My treatment was also delayed because the doctors wanted clear X-rays, but my bones were so fractured that the X-rays were cloudy. Finally I got three pints of blood, a tracheotomy and a bed.

I slept deeply. I remember trying to wake up, aware that I was in a bed with sheets. But something was wrong. I struggled to open my swollen eyes, only to discover ants crawling on my nose and many more trailing across my bed and body. I got the orderly's attention by standing up. While he helped me, I caught a glimpse of a mirror and needed to look twice to be sure that it was really me. The reflected face was swollen beyond recognition, and my eye whites were blood red. My lower jaw was shattered. Below my nose was a gaping hole. I must have been in denial because all I wanted to know was how long it would be until I could rejoin my unit.

After a week, life in the ward became routine. The Quonset hut held maybe 12 beds. A television at one end droned on, and three loud and chatty NVA soldiers kept me nervous by their presence. For days I watched one GI who was determined to die. He would thrash about, and when conscious he would rip off his bandages and fight off the staff. One afternoon I saw him relax; then he crunched his head to his left shoulder and let go of life. He was dead.

Ten days after being hit I was flown to Japan. One week later I was again airborne, reading the Stars and Stripes article about my fellow soldiers' battle:

At least 77 Communists' bodies were left on the battlefield at

Defending LZ Grant

Landing Zone Grant, a brush-covered plain in the shadow of Mt. Nui Ba Den, about 15 miles northeast of Tay Ninh City.

There were indications that well over 100 Reds had died in the midnight fight but that the survivors had carried many bodies away.

The fighting began at the landing zone moments after a heavy mortar barrage. One huge 120mm-mortar shell crashed through the roof of the operations center, killing the camp commander and three others.

Seven other GIs died and 30 were wounded defending the landing zone.

Although some Communists carried flame-throwers, apparently none got close enough to use them. Two of the napalm-loaded weapons were captured, along with a small anti-aircraft gun and scores of other weapons used in the attack.

Maj. Billy Brown, 30, who took command of the camp after the commander was killed, said the rifle company that defended the camp fought so well that most of the Claymore mines ringing the camp were not needed and were not fired.

Air strikes and Spooky gun-ships peppered the Reds as they charged and the camp's defenders lowered their artillery pieces and fired point blank into the on-rushing Reds.

At least six Communists made it through two rings of concertina barbed wire to die less than 30 feet from the guns of the cavalry troopers. None made it through the final defenses.

We landed at Travis Air Force Base in Oakland, Calif., on the afternoon of March 12, 1969. The hospital policy was to offer a free phone call home and a steak dinner for each new returnee. The dinner and phone were placed in front of every patient. I stared at that little steak for a long time. The next day we flew on a hospital shuttle to cities within California. After many stops, we passed over familiar-looking eucalyptus trees as we approached Miramar Naval Air Station, San Diego.

Miramar was only a few miles from my family's ranch near Del Mar. Balboa Naval Hospital in downtown San Diego became my home for the next year. I had many 30-day leaves for recuperation from surgeries. In a series of operations the great Navy doctors reconstructed my lower jaw and moved my face around to cover lost tissues. Once I looked pretty good I was transferred to San Pedro Army Hospital, where I was discharged on April 7, 1970, with a 60 percent disability rating.

In 1973 I was back in Balboa for yet another surgery when the recently released American POWs arrived. Each ex-prisoner was driven to the hospital door in a limousine. About 200 proud and raucous sailors and patients welcomed them. I was right there, yelling my heart out.

In 1999, as the 30th anniversary of my tour in Vietnam neared, I finally decided to contact my fellow cannoneer in the 77th Artillery, George Presson. He lived in Ferndale, Calif. We hadn't spoken since LZ Grant, but I phoned him, recognized his voice and told him my name. "Fisher," he said, "I think about you every day." I held our conversation to a minimum because I wanted to speak to him in person. With his address in hand, I drove for a full day to Ferndale.

I found Presson to be still squared-away and strong of mind and body. During his tour in Vietnam he had earned two Purple Hearts and three Army Commendation Medals, two with "V" devices for valor. I am grateful for his assistance in writing this article.

Vietnam Magazine
June, 2006 Issue
By Weider History Group
www.TheHistoryNet.com

12/5/1972... Del Mar had its one and only anti-war protest at which Fisher was arrested. The seven time mayor of Del Mar (seen in the crutches) attempts to stop the violent arrests. This was also Fishers one and only anti-war protest.

The Living Ghosts

Howard standing in the sand at Del Mar, 1976

"I was introduced to John Morton in the summer of 2021 and after exchanging my book he agreed to let me use his great poem 'Epic of Recon Team Krait' to end my books content with the poem on the last page. It's the impact of this poem on Memorial Day and indeed Veteran's Day that hits American's in their heart. A big salute to John Morton - WIA at LZ X-Ray (La Drang Valley), 14th November, 1965 and again 15th November, 1965 and finally again 7th February, 1969 - recon team.

14th Nov, 1965 - Shrapnel in butt from AK fire through belly of UH-ID.
15th Nov, 1965 - AK bullet through right leg while serving as crew chief with 229th on UH-ID. Major Bruce Crandall our C.O.
7th Feb, 1969 - Read the poem on the last page about this day."
    -Howard Fisher

The Living Ghosts

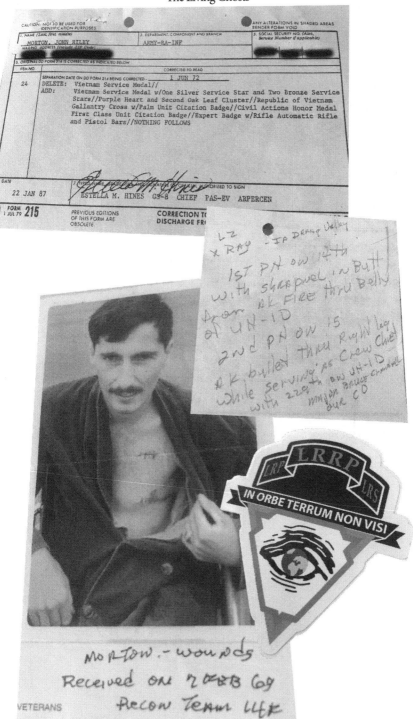

'Epic of Recon Team Krait'

Bullet in my shoulder, three more in my chest, my recon team has met its fate, we've tried our very best.

AK fire comes quickly, like shadows in the night, the lives are snuffed from three brave men, the next turn comes mine.

A rustle in the bushes, the VC are very near, then explosives from my CAR-15 and they fall amongst the gear.

My life is flashed before my eyes, my time is near its end, the ground is stained crimson red, the facts of war are grim.

My strength is slowly leaving, the time has almost come, why must so many young men die, so very far from home?

Then suddenly from Heaven, like angels from above, a Medivac and two gunships appear before my eyes.

All hell breaks loose around me, the enemy turns to run, a sweet long burst from the guns above and the tides of war are turned.

The smell of death still lingers, the medics flock around, my life is plucked from the gates of hell, another time will come.

At half the flags are flying, bugles in the air, a tribute to all my friends, who gave with will their all.

by Riley Morton
LRRP Team Leader
75th Rangers

Howard Fisher received the Army Commendation Metal with "V" device for his actions at LZ Grant. After his release from the army he worked for the city of Del Mar, Calif. He currently resides in Julian, Calif. with his two dogs and is often visited by his three sons Weston, Travis, and Chase.

To contact Howard Fisher please write to:

Howard Fisher
PO Box 406
Santa Ysabel, CA 92070

Email: hfwynola@gmail.com

Or find him on Social Media.

Made in the USA
Las Vegas, NV
11 April 2023